Instructor's Manual and Test Bank

to accompany

Health Psychology

Fourth Edition

Shelley E. Taylor
University of California at Los Angeles

Prepared by
Cheryl A. Rickabaugh
University of Redlands

 **McGraw-Hill College**

Boston   Burr Ridge, IL   Dubuque, IA   Madison, WI   New York   San Francisco   St. Louis
Bangkok   Bogotá   Caracas   Lisbon   London   Madrid
Mexico City   Milan   New Delhi   Seoul   Singapore   Sydney   Taipei   Toronto

McGraw-Hill College

A Division of The McGraw-Hill Companies

Instructor's Manual and Test Bank to accompany
HEALTH PSYCHOLOGY, FOURTH EDITION

4 5 6 7 8 9 0 QPD/QPD 9 3 2 1 0

ISBN 0-07-292747-X

www.mhhe.com

CONTENTS

iv

PREFACE

The primary purpose of this manual is to provide a framework to assist instructors, particularly those who may be teaching this course for the first time, in the preparation of lectures, classroom activities, and objective test items for use with *Health Psychology*, Fourth Edition, by Shelley E. Taylor. Each chapter of this manual includes a chapter outline, learning objectives, lecture suggestions, classroom activities, recommended reading for students, ten true-false questions, and forty-five multiple-choice questions. Five essay questions per chapter have been added for this edition of this text.

The outlines and learning objectives provide an overview of each textbook chapter at a glance. The lecture suggestions expand upon topics introduced in the text or introduce additional topics that complement the text material. Complete references accompany each lecture suggestion to make it easier for instructors to locate sources.

I have also attempted to include at least one activity suitable for in-class demonstrations or outside projects for students. Each of these suggestions has been used in my classes, and they have proven to be useful techniques to encourage student involvement. Many of the outside projects suggested in this manual are accompanied by a sample assignment. These assignments may be used in their present form or modified to suit individual needs or preferences.

The range of recommended readings reflects, I hope, the diversity of students who are interested in courses in health psychology. I have attempted to include readings that are suitable for students with a minimal background in psychology, for students training to become practitioners in the field, and for advanced students who may already be working in the health care delivery system.

Finally, the true-false, multiple choice, and essay questions have been written to follow the text's topical progression. The questions include both factual and applied questions of important concepts as well as identification/definition of important terms. The correct answer for each question is underscored, and the relevant pages of the text are referenced.

CHAPTER 1
WHAT IS HEALTH PSYCHOLOGY?

Chapter Outline

I. Definitions of Health Psychology

II. The Mind-Body Relationship: A Brief History

III. Why Is the Field of Health Psychology Needed?

    A. Changing Patterns of Illness

    B. Expanded Health Care Services

    C. Increased Medical Acceptance

    D. Demonstrated Contributions to Health

    E. Methodological Contributions

IV. The Biopsychosocial Model in Health Psychology

    A. The Biopsychosocial Model Versus the Biomedical Model

    B. Advantages of the Biopsychosocial Model

    C. Clinical Implications of the Biopsychosocial Model

V. What Is Health Psychology Training For?

Learning Objectives

1. Define health psychology.

2. Describe the changing philosophical perspectives on the mind-body relationship from the time of ancient cultures to the present day.

3. Summarize the criticisms of the psychosomatic movement.

4. Explain the factors that have contributed to the rise of health psychology.

5. Describe changing patterns of illness in the United States.

6. Describe trends in the expansion of health care services in the United States.

7. Describe the research methodologies employed by health psychologists.

8. Compare and contrast the biopsychosocial model and biomedical models of health. Summarize the advantages of the biopsychosocial model.

9. Describe how systems theory explains the interaction of biopsychosocial variables.

10. Describe the clinical implications of the biopsychosocial model.

11. Describe the different occupations that employ health psychologists.

Lecture Suggestions

Measurement Issues

The measurement of health-related outcomes is often a difficult and subjective task. The adoption of the biopsychosocial model of health assumes that any assessment of health must take into account the physiological state of the subject as well as any psychosocial distress he or she may experience. Thus, evaluating the efficacy of a medical treatment or intervention by use of traditional health-related outcomes or criteria often may be problematic. For example, the quality of life becomes an important issue when a biomedical criterion such as life expectancy (the number of years the subject may be expected to live based on the age-specific death rate of the birth cohort) is adopted in assessing health-related outcomes. Similar concerns are expressed by those who criticize the use of mortality rates (the proportion of deaths within a population) and morbidity rates (the number of years free from disease) as outcome measures. Thus, alternative measures such as functional status, which typically is represented as a composite measure of a person's physical abilities, cognitive abilities, role involvement, etc., may become increasingly useful.

Evans, D. R. (1997). Health promotion, wellness programs, quality of life and the marketing of psychology. Canadian Psychology, 38, 1–12.

Karoly, P. (Ed.). (1985). Measurement strategies in health psychology. New York: Wiley.

Levy, J. A., Jasmin, C., & Bez, G. (Ed.) (1997). Cancer, AIDS, and quality of life. New York, Plenum Press.

Streufert, S., & Streufert, S. C. (1982). Experimentation in behavioral medicine: In search of an applicable method. In J. R. Eiser (Ed.), Social psychology and behavioral medicine, (pp. 63–76). Chichester: Wiley.

The Biopsychosocial Model

The text's presentation of the biopsychosocial model may be developed by discussing the role of environmental variables that affect health and illness. Taylor, Repetti, and Seeman's (1997) review describes the way in which community, work, family, and peer environments contribute to chronic and acute illness. This review also serves as an introduction to topics addressed in subsequent chapters (e.g., health behaviors, stress, and coping).

Taylor, S. E., Repetti, R. L., & Seeman, T. (1997). Health psychology: What is an unhealthy environment and how does it get under the skin? In J. T. Spence, J. M. Darley, & D. J. Foss (Eds.), Annual review of psychology (Vol. 48, pp. 411–447). Palo Alto, CA: Annual Reviews.

Exercises, Projects, and Activities

Health Psychology in the Popular Press

Have students bring to class articles from the news media and the popular press about health issues to discuss in class. Many newspapers have a weekly health section, and a number of magazines devoted to health, fitness, and wellness are readily available. These news items may provide the basis for a discussion of the transmission of research findings to the general population, the problems in interpreting research in health psychology, and the frustrations experienced by media consumers who may have to sift through a series of competing health-related claims.

Research Methods in Health Psychology

The exercise described above may be modified to provide an opportunity for students to apply the research methods adopted by health psychologists in specific instances. Organize students into groups of three to four members and distribute a different newspaper or magazine article that makes a health-related claim to each group. Articles may be readily found in health-related magazines (e.g., Prevention, Self), general interest magazines (e.g., Reader's Digest, Redbook), and local newspapers. Ask students to devise a research study that would test the claims in the media report they have been assigned. Students generally can outline a research study within 30 minutes. Have them report their studies to the class for peer critique.

Recommended Reading

Resnick, R. J., & Rozensky, R. H. (Eds.). (1997). Health psychology through the life span: Practice and research opportunities. Washington, DC: American Psychological Association.

This book provides a current survey of clinical and research issues in health psychology. Chapters address the role of health psychology in the health care delivery system, the role of psychologists in medical care settings, and disease control and management.

Kiple, K. F. (Ed.). (1993). The Cambridge world history of human disease. Cambridge: Cambridge University Press.

This edited volume documents the history of medicine and disease from a cross-cultural perspective. It also contains sections devoted to changing conceptions of health and disease, issues in health measurement, and major human diseases.

True-False Questions

1. <u>T</u>   F   The 1948 World Health Organization's definition of health is analogous to a state of wellness. (ref. p. 3)

2. T   <u>F</u>   Early cultures took a dualistic approach to the mind and the body. (ref. p. 4)

3. <u>T</u>   F   Trephination is a procedure practiced by early cultures that involved drilling a small hole in the skull to allow evil spirits to leave the body. (ref. p. 4)

4. <u>T</u>   F   In conversion hysteria, the patient converts psychological conflict into a symptom which then relieves the patient of anxiety. (ref. p. 5)

5. T   <u>F</u>   The most important factor giving rise to health psychology has been the expansion of health care services. (ref. p. 7)

6. <u>T</u>   F   Morbidity may be expressed in two ways: as the number of new cases or as the total number of existing cases of an illness. (ref. p. 8)

7. T   <u>F</u>   Although health psychologists have been employed in health settings for many years, they have difficulty establishing their credibility with physicians and other health care professionals. (ref. p. 10)

8. <u>T</u>   F   One advantage of correlational studies is the ability to study health-related variables in situations where random assignment is impractical. (ref. p. 11)

9.   T   <u>F</u>   The biomedical model emphasizes health over illness. (ref. p. 12)

10. <u>T</u>   F   The biopsychosocial model emphasizes the importance of an effective patient-practitioner relationship. (ref. p. 14)

Multiple-Choice Questions

1.   The field within psychology devoted to understanding all psychological influences on health and illness across the life span is called (ref. p. 3)
     a.   psychosomatic medicine
     <u>b</u>.   health psychology
     c.   medical psychology
     d.   epidemiology

2.   Which of the following is **not** a focus of health psychology? (ref. p. 4)
     a.   health promotion and maintenance
     b.   etiology and correlates of health and illness
     c.   the health care system
     <u>d</u>.   none of the above

3.   Ancient cultures viewed the mind and the body to be (ref. p. 4)
     a.   ultimately unknowable
     b.   somewhat interdependent
     c.   separate and autonomous systems
     <u>d</u>.   part of the same system

4.   According to the humoral theory of Hippocrates and Galen, disease is the result of (ref. p. 4)
     a.   trephination
     b.   evil spirits
     <u>c</u>.   an imbalance of bodily fluids
     d.   cellular disorders

5.   The idea that one's biochemistry may be associated with certain personality characteristics can be traced to the (ref. p. 4)
     a.   Stone Age
     <u>b</u>.   ancient Greeks
     c.   Middle Ages
     d.   Renaissance

6.   A tribal shaman chants and burns herbs over a woman's body in order to drive out the evil spirits which are thought to be causing her seizures. The shaman is practicing (ref. p. 4)
     a.   trephination
     <u>b</u>.   demonology
     c.   psychosomatic medicine
     d.   dualistic medicine

7. According to the theory of cellular pathology (ref. p. 4)
   a. the mind and body function as a unit
   b. illness can be traced to biological disorders
   c. social factors may also play a minor role in disease
   d. psychological pathology may be manifested in physical disorders

8. Conversion hysteria (ref. p. 5)
   a. is now even more frequent than in Freud's time
   b. occurs when unconscious conflict is manifested in a symbolic physical symptom
   c. occurs when an individual develops a number of minor symptoms in order to avoid interpersonal conflict
   d. all of the above

9. _____ linked specific personality patterns to specific illnesses. (ref. p. 5–6)
   a. Dunbar and Alexander
   b. Galen
   c. Hippocrates
   d. Freud

10. According to the perspective of psychosomatic medicine, certain disorders are caused by (ref. p. 6)
    a. emotional conflict
    b. an imbalance of bodily fluids
    c. organic pathology
    d. social factors

11. Which of the following is **not** a criticism of psychosomatic medicine? (ref. p. 6)
    a. Much of the work on which many of the disorder profiles were based suffers from methodological problems.
    b. There is no scientific evidence that a particular psychological conflict or personality type is sufficient to produce illness.
    c. None of the early ideas generated by the psychosomatic medicine perspective have had a lasting influence upon health psychology.
    d. The psychosomatic movement restricted the range of medical problems to which psychological and social factors might apply.

12. The field of health psychology has been greatly influenced by the psychosomatic movement. Which of the following assumptions of this movement has made a lasting contribution to health psychology? (ref. p. 6)
    a. Psychological conflict is sufficient to produce certain disorders.
    b. Certain biological disorders can be related on a consistent basis to specific personality types.
    c. Certain disorders are best treated medically; however, other disorders are best treated through psychotherapy.
    d. Physical health is affected by both the psychological and social environment.

13. Until the turn of the century, _____ were the major causes of illness and death in the United States. (ref. p. 7)
    a. acute disorders
    b. chronic illnesses
    c. hereditary disorders
    d. accidents and homicides

14. Considering the most prevalent causes of death today, the most effective preventive measures would include (ref. p. 7)
    a. mass public immunization programs
    b. lifestyle management
    c. adding nutritional supplements to foods (e.g., vitamin D in milk)
    d. all of the above

15. Acute disorders are (ref. p. 7)
    a. short-term medical illnesses that are usually amenable to cure
    b. typically diseases that are co-managed by patients and their practitioners
    c. the major causes of death and illness in the United States
    d. serious disorders such as heart disease, cancer, and diabetes

16. Chronic illnesses (ref. p. 7)
    a. are illnesses that are psychosomatic in origin
    b. are difficult for patients to manage, but seldom contribute to disability or death
    c. can be cured only if the patient and the practitioner work together as a team
    d. are illnesses in which psychological and social factors play an important role in both cause and management

17. Today's college students are more likely to die from _____ than _____ . (ref. p. 7)
    a. infections; acute disorders
    b. pneumonia; diabetes
    c. heart disease; pneumonia
    d. acute disorders; chronic illness

18. Which of the following was listed as the most frequent cause of death in 1994? (ref. p. 7)
    a. Cerebrovascular disease (stroke)
    b. Heart disease
    c. Cancer
    d. Influenza and pneumonia

19. _____ is the study of the frequency, distribution, and causes of infectious and non-infectious disease in a population, based on an investigation of the physical and social environment. (ref. p. 8)
    a. Health psychology
    b. Etiology
    c. Morbidity
    d. Epidemiology

20. _____ refers to the number of cases of a disease that exist at some given point in time. _____ refers to the number of deaths due to particular causes. (ref. p. 8)

    a. Morbidity; Mortality
    b. Mortality; Morbidity
    c. Epidemiology; Pathogen
    d. Etiology; Epidemiology

21. Health psychologists interested in issues related to quality of life are likely to be most interested in which of the following? (ref. p. 9)

    a. prevalence of acute illnesses in the population
    b. mortality statistics
    c. morbidity statistics
    d. none of the above

22. Americans spend more than _____ of their total income on health care. (ref. p. 9)

    a. 5%
    b. 14%
    c. 25%
    d. 30%

23. Which of the following is **not** listed as one of health psychology's contributions to the expansion of health care services in the United States? (ref. p. 9)

    a. The emphasis on prevention and the modification of health-compromising behaviors which encourages cost containment.
    b. Research on patient satisfaction with treatment which assists in the design of user-friendly health care systems.
    c. Health psychologists' primary role in administering tests and interpreting test results of psychologically disturbed patients.
    d. None of the above.

24. Random assignment is an important characteristic of (ref. p. 10)

    a. experiments
    b. correlational research
    c. longitudinal research
    d. all of the above

25. Dr. Garcia has recently completed a study of personality and physical health. He administered a questionnaire to college students that included a standardized optimism scale and a symptom checklist. He found that participants with higher levels of optimism reported fewer physical symptoms. This is an example of a(n) (ref. p. 11)

    a. experiment
    b. correlational research
    c. prospective research
    d. retrospective research

26. The disadvantages of correlational research are remedied by the use of (ref. p. 11)

    a. experiments
    b. prospective research
    c. longitudinal research
    d. all of the above

27. Correlational studies have advantages over experiments because they allow one to (ref. p. 11)
   a. determine the direction of causality
   b. study variables that may not be manipulated
   c. rule out the influence of co-occurring variables
   d. all of the above

28. Dr. Yee has taken the medical histories of 30 women who have the symptoms of a chronic illness. She is identifying factors in these histories that these patients share that have contributed to the development of their current illness. This is an example of a(n): (ref. p. 11)
   a. experiment
   b. prospective research
   c. retrospective research
   d. none of the above

29. _____ assesses the extent to which a group of individuals or a relationship between two variable changes over time. (ref. p. 11)
   a. Experiments
   b. Prospective research
   c. Retrospective research
   d. none of the above

30. An observed correlation between hostility and cardiovascular disease allows one to conclude that (ref. p. 11)
   a. higher levels of hostility are linked to increased incidence of cardiovascular disease
   b. risk factors for cardiovascular disease are linked to higher levels of hostility
   c. some other factors might be associated with the development of both cardiovascular disease and hostility
   d. all of the above are plausible explanations for the correlation

31. Medical practitioners increasingly recognize that psychological and social factors play an important role in health and illness. This suggests that (ref. p. 12)
   a. dualism is becoming increasingly accepted
   b. the biopsychosocial model is becoming increasingly accepted
   c. practitioners now are more likely to refer problem patients to psychiatrists
   d. practitioners now are more likely to refer healthy patients to psychologists

32. The biomedical model is associated with (ref. p. 12)
   a. psychosomatic medicine
   b. dualism
   c. the mind-body relationship
   d. macrolevel processes

33. The idea that illness can be explained by the functions of disordered cells and chemical imbalances is (ref. p. 12)
    a. dualism
    b. systems theory
    c. homeostasis
    d. reductionism

34. The notion that cancer can be cured simply by excising a tumor most closely resembles the (ref. p. 12)
    a. biomedical model
    b. biopsychosocial model
    c. psychosomatic model
    d. pathological model

35. The idea that health is the absence of disease most closely resembles the (ref. p. 12)
    a. biomedical model
    b. biopsychosocial model
    c. psychosomatic model
    d. pathological model

36. A single-factor model of illness assumes that (ref. p. 12)
    a. there is one ultimate cause of all illnesses
    b. health should be emphasized over illness
    c. illness can be explained in terms of biological disorder
    d. all of the above

37. The _____ emphasizes illness over health. (ref. p. 12)
    a. biopsychosocial model
    b. psychosomatic model
    c. reductionistic model
    d. biomedical model

38. According to the biomedical model, a person is ill when (ref. p. 12)
    a. symptoms are first perceived
    b. the sick role is assumed
    c. biological systems become disordered
    d. none of the above

39. The biomedical model fails to explain how (ref. pp. 12–13)
    a. a viral infection can be successfully treated by antibiotics
    b. a headache can be relieved by aspirin
    c. a toothache can be successfully treated with a root canal
    d. chronic pain can be relieved with a sugar pill

40. According to the biopsychosocial model, health and illness are determined by (ref. p. 12–13)
    a. microlevel processes
    b. macrolevel processes
    c. an interaction of microlevel and macrolevel processes
    d. none of the above

41. An example of a macrolevel process that affects illness is the effect of (ref. p. 13)
   a. nicotine on the lung tissues
   b. depression on recovery from surgery
   c. long-term exposure to toxic waste on a region's cancer rate
   d. antibiotics on infection

42. Systems theory assumes a principle of hierarchical organization. This implies that (ref. p. 13)
   a. changes in any one level will affect all other levels of the system
   b. only changes in the highest level will affect all levels of the system
   c. changes in one level will affect only lower levels of the system
   d. changes in intermediate levels have the most profound impacts

43. Taking a systems theory approach to health and illness involves (ref. p. 13)
   a. collaboration among medical and social science professionals
   b. interdisciplinary approaches to problems
   c. looking at the individual's medical condition within a psychosocial context
   d. all of the above

44. According to the biopsychosocial model, (ref. p. 14)
   a. an interdisciplinary team approach may lead to the best diagnoses
   b. treatment must focus on biological, psychological, and social factors
   c. patients play an important role in their diagnosis and treatment
   d. all of the above

45. Health psychologists typically are employed (ref. pp. 14–15)
   a. in academic settings where they conduct research programs in health psychology
   b. by public agencies such as the Centers for Disease Control
   c. as clinicians who work with medical patients
   d. all of the above

Essay Questions

1. Explain the principles that characterize the psychosomatic movement. In what ways has the psychosomatic movement influenced the practice of health psychology? (ref. p. 6)

2. Explain how changing patterns of illness have contributed to the rise of health psychology. (ref. pp. 7–8)

3. Explain how prospective and retrospective research remedies the problems of correlational research. (ref. p. 11)

4. Design an experiment and a correlational study to test this hypothesis: People who consume moderate levels of alcohol are at lower risk of heart disease. Explain the advantages and disadvantages of each methodology. (ref. p. 11)

5. Compare and contrast the biopsychosocial and biomedical models. Include in your explanation the advantages of the biopsychosocial model over the biomedical model. (ref. pp. 12–13).

CHAPTER 2
THE SYSTEMS OF THE BODY

Chapter Outline

I.   The Nervous System

    A.   Overview

    B.   The Brain

        1.   The Hindbrain and the Midbrain

        2.   The Forebrain

        3.   The Reticular Activating System and the Limbic System

    C.   The Spinal Cord

    D.   The Autonomic Nervous System

    E.   The Role of Neurotransmitters

    F.   Disorders of the Nervous System

        1.   Epilepsy

        2.   Cerebral Palsy

        3.   Parkinson's Disease

        4.   Multiple Sclerosis

        5.   Myasthenia Gravis

        6.   Huntington's Disease

II.   The Endocrine System

    A.   Overview

    B.   The Adrenal Glands

    C.   Diabetes

III. The Cardiovascular System

    A.   Overview

    B.   The Heart

    C.   Diseases of the Cardiovascular System

VI.   The Renal System

    A.   Overview

    B.   Disorders of the Renal System

VII.   The Reproductive System and an Introduction to Genetics

    A.   The Ovaries and Testes

    B.   Fertilization and Gestation

        1.   Disorders of the Reproductive System

    C.   Genetics and Health

        1.   Genetics and Psychology

VIII.   The Immune System

    A.   The Course of Infection

    B.   Immunity

        1.   Nonspecific Immunity

        2.   Specific Immunity

        3.   The Lymphatic System's Role in Immunity

    C.   Diseases of the Immune System

Learning Objectives

1. Identify and describe the structure of the nervous system.

2. Identify and describe the structure and function of the peripheral nervous system.

3. Identify and describe the structure and function of the autonomic nervous system.

4. Differentiate between the sympathetic and parasympathetic nervous systems and describe their functions.

5. Identify and describe the three sections that comprise the human brain.

6. Differentiate between the medulla, pons, and cerebellum and describe their functions.

7. Describe the functions of the midbrain.

8. Describe the structure of the forebrain.

9. Differentiate between the thalamus and the hypothalamus and describe their functions.

10. Describe the structure and functions of the four lobes comprising the cerebral cortex.

11. Describe the structure and functions of the reticular activating system and the limbic system.

12. Describe the structure and functions of the spinal cord and identify common disorders of the spinal cord.

13. Describe the structure and functions of the sympathetic and parasympathetic nervous systems.

14. Describe the nature and functions of neurotransmitters.

15. Identify and describe the common disorders of the nervous system.

16. Describe the structure and functions of the endocrine system.

17. Describe the functions of the adrenal glands and their role in the endocrine system.

18. Describe the nature of diabetes, differentiating between Type I and Type II diabetes.

19. Describe the structure and function of the cardiovascular system.

20. Describe the structure and function of the heart and identify common diseases of the cardiovascular system.

21. Describe the factors that influence blood pressure. Identify common blood-related disorders.

22. Describe the structure and function of the respiratory system and identify common respiratory system disorders.

23. Describe the structure and function of the digestive system and identify common digestive system disorders.

24. Describe the structure and function of the renal system and identify common disorders of the renal system.

25. Describe the structure and function of the male and female reproductive systems.

26. Explain the processes of fertilization and gestation.

27. Identify common disorders of the reproductive system.

28. Explain the inheritance of susceptibility to disease, and describe the role of psychology in genetics.

29. Describe the structure and function of the immune system.

30. Describe the routes of disease transmission and the course of infection.

31. Describe the nature of immunity and differentiate between nonspecific and specific immune mechanisms.

32. Describe the role of the lymphatic system in immunity.

33. Identify common disorders of the immune system.

Lecture Suggestions

Genetic Counseling

This chapter's introduction to reproduction and genetics may be supplemented by introducing psychological issues in genetic counseling. Emery and Pullen (1984) provide an overview of genetic disorders and counseling techniques. Chapter topics that are relevant to health psychology include mental and physical disorders, late onset disorders (e.g., Huntington's disease), sterilization, artificial insemination, and prenatal diagnoses. In addition, Baum, Friedman, and Zakowski (1997) describe the benefits as well as the potential for psychological distress that may accompany risk analysis. This particular issue (January,

1997) of Health Psychology addresses psychological aspects of genetic testing that may be incorporated into lecture topics for this and subsequent chapters.

Baum, A., Friedman, A. L., & Zakowski, S. G. (1997). Stress and genetic testing for disease risk. Health Psychology, 16, 8–19.

Emery, A. E. H., & Pullen, I. M. (Eds.). (1984). Psychological aspects of genetic counseling. London: Academic Press.

Recommended Reading

Ornstein, R., & Sobel, D. (1987). The healing brain. New York: Simon and Schuster.

This popular book provides an introduction to the basic concepts of psychosomatic medicine and the relationship of psychological states to physical health.

Ornstein, R., & Swencionis, C. (Eds.). (1990). The healing brain: A scientific reader. New York: Guilford Press.

The editors present an advanced discussion of the relationship of the brain and psychological factors to physical health. Chapter topics include psychosocial factors in healing; environmental influences on physical health; and introduction to psychoneuroimmunology, processes in bodily regulation, and coping with stress.

Restak, R. M. (1995). Brainscapes: An introduction to what neuroscience has learned about the structure, function, and abilities of the brain. New York: Hyperion.

This popular book describes the structure and function of the brain and the medical technology used in diagnosing neurological disorders.

True-False Questions

1. <u>T</u>   F   Regulation of the autonomic nervous system occurs via the sympathetic nervous system and the parasympathetic nervous system. (ref. pp. 17–18)

2. <u>T</u>   F   The structures of the limbic system play an important role in the experience of emotion. (ref. p. 20)

3. T   <u>F</u>   The parasympathetic nervous system is activated in individual responses to stress. (ref. p. 21)

4. <u>T</u>   F   The most common forms of neurological dysfunction are epilepsy and Parkinson's disease. (ref. p. 22)

5. T   <u>F</u>   Cholesterol deposits are implicated in the development of arteriosclerosis . (ref. p. 28)

6. <u>T</u>   F   Hepatitis B is typically transmitted through food and water. (ref. p. 37)

7. <u>T</u>   F   Women who have contracted several sexually transmitted diseases are at risk of developing chronic pelvic inflammatory disease. (ref. p. 40)

8. <u>T</u>   F   There appears to be a genetic contribution to coronary heart disease and some forms of cancer. (ref. p. 41)

9. T   <u>F</u>   Antigens are proteins produced in response to stimulation by antibodies. (ref. p. 45)

10. T   <u>F</u>   Compared to women, men are at greater risk of contracting autoimmune disease. (ref. p. 47)

Multiple-Choice Questions

1. The nervous system as a whole consists of the ____ and the ____ . (ref. p. 17)
    a. brain; spinal cord
    <u>b.</u> central nervous system; peripheral nervous system
    c. somatic nervous system; autonomic nervous system
    d. sensory nervous system; motor nervous system

2. The peripheral nervous system consists of the _____ and the _____. (ref. p. 17)
    a. brain; spinal cord
    b. central nervous system; peripheral nervous system
    <u>c.</u> somatic nervous system; autonomic nervous system
    d. forebrain; hindbrain

3. Damage to the cerebellum is associated with impaired (ref. pp. 18–19)
    <u>a.</u> muscular coordination
    b. respiration
    c. speech
    d. visual acuity

4. Which of the following is **not** a function of the hypothalamus? (ref. p. 19)
    a. control of cardiac functioning, blood pressure, and respiration
    b. regulation of the endocrine system
    <u>c.</u> transmission of sensory impulses to the cerebral cortex
    d. regulation of hunger, thirst, and sexual arousal

5. June was involved in an automobile accident in which she suffered extensive damage to the cerebral cortex. Since the accident, she has experienced difficulty in coordinating voluntary movement. In particular, June has difficulty in controlling activities on the right side of her body. June most likely suffered damage in the (ref. p. 20)
    <u>a.</u> left frontal lobe
    b. right frontal lobe
    c. left parietal lobe
    d. right parietal lobe

6. The reticular activating system is responsible for the (ref. p. 20)
    a. interpretation of emotional experience
    b. activation of smooth, orderly muscle contractions
    <u>c.</u> activation of the brain for incoming afferent impulses
    d. none of the above

7. The sympathetic nervous system (ref. p. 21)
   a. is an anabolic system
   b. is a central part of the somatic nervous system
   c. plays an important role in reactions to stress
   d. all of the above

8. The _____ nervous system mobilizes the body in response to stress; the _____ nervous system controls the activities of the visceral organs under normal conditions. (ref. p. 21)
   a. parasympathetic; sympathetic
   b. sympathetic; parasympathetic
   c. somatic; autonomic
   d. autonomic; peripheral

9. _____ is a chronic, nonprogressive disorder of the nervous system that is marked by lack of muscle control. (ref. p. 22)
   a. Epilepsy
   b. Parkinson's disease
   c. Myasthenia gravis
   d. Multiple sclerosis

10. The gene for _____ was recently isolated which allows for at-risk individuals to be tested to ascertain whether they are carriers of this hereditary disorder characterized by chronic physical and mental deterioration due to damaged brain cells. (ref. p. 23)
    a. Epilepsy
    b. Myasthenia gravis
    c. Multiple sclerosis
    d. Huntington's disease

11. The nervous system is chiefly responsible for _____ responses to changes in the body; whereas the endocrine system governs mainly _____ responses. (ref. p. 23)
    a. fast-acting, short-duration; slow-acting, long-duration
    b. slow-acting, long-duration; fast-acting, short-duration
    c. fast-acting, long-duration; slow-acting, short-duration
    d. complementary; antagonistic

12. The endocrine system (ref. pp. 23–24)
    a. regulates the secretion of neurotransmitters and corticosteroids
    b. plays a critical role in reactions to stress
    c. helps regulate growth
    d. all of the above

13. The release of corticosteroids via the adrenal cortex is regulated by (ref. p. 24)
    a. epinephrine and norepinephrine
    b. glucocorticoids
    c. thyrotropic hormone (TSH)
    d. adrenocorticotropic hormone (ACTH)

14. Secretion of catecholamines (ref. p. 24)
    a. increases protein and fat mobilization
    b. regulates sodium retention
    c. increases heart rate and blood pressure
    d. all of the above

15. Type I diabetes (ref. pp. 24–25)
    a. typically occurs after age 40
    b. is a condition that occurs when the body fails to produce enough insulin
    c. is a condition that occurs when the body is not sufficiently responsive to insulin
    d. is primarily managed through dietary and exercise regimens

16. Conditions associated with diabetes include (ref. pp. 25–26)
    a. hypoglycemia
    b. hyperglycemia
    c. coronary heart disease
    d. all of the above

17. The _____ carry blood from the heart to oxygenate organs and other tissues. (ref. p. 26)
    a. arteries
    b. veins
    c. capillaries
    d. all of the above

18. During _____, blood is pumped out of the heart, and blood pressure _____ . During _____, blood is taken into the heart, and blood pressure _____. (ref. p. 26)
    a. diastole; increases; systole; decreases
    b. diastole; decreases; systole; increases
    c. systole; increases; diastole; decreases
    d. systole; decreases; diastole; increases

19. Atherosclerosis is (ref. p. 28)
    a. associated with angina pectoris and myocardial infarction
    b. characterized by a hardening and reduced elasticity of the arterial walls
    c. a hereditary disease rather than a disease of lifestyle
    d. none of the above

20. Approximately 55% of blood volume is composed of (ref. p. 29)
    a. platelets
    b. white blood cells
    c. red blood cells
    d. plasma

21. Lymphocytes play an important role in fighting infection and disease by (ref. p. 29)
    a. secreting digesting enzymes that dissolve foreign particles
    b. producing antibodies that destroy substances through the antigen-antibody reaction
    c. secreting platelets that engulf foreign particles so they may be excreted
    d. producing monoblasts that increase the amount of hemoglobin in the blood

22. Some individuals are unable to produce thromboplastin and fibrin. This condition is associated with a clotting disorder called (ref. p. 31)
    a. arteriosclerosis
    b. anemia
    c. leukopenia
    d. hemophilia

23. The exchange of oxygen and carbon dioxide during respiration occurs between the (ref. p. 31)
    a. bronchi and the capillaries
    b. alveoli and the capillaries
    c. alveoli and the arteries
    d. bronchioles and the alveoli

24. _____ involves a condition in which the alveoli become dilated, atrophied, and thin so that elasticity is lost and exhalation becomes difficult. (ref. p. 34)
    a. Bronchial pneumonia
    b. Pleurisy
    c. Tuberculosis
    d. Pulmonary emphysema

25. During the digestive process, the absorption of food takes place primarily in the (ref. p. 35)
    a. stomach
    b. duodenum
    c. small intestine
    d. large intestine

26. The pancreas plays an important role in digestion because it is responsible for the secretion of (ref. p. 35)
    a. bile
    b. insulin
    c. pepsin
    d. bolus

27. Both Hepatitis A and Hepatitis B are (ref. pp. 36–37)
    a. caused by viruses
    b. transmitted through food and water
    c. transmitted through blood or IV needles
    d. none of the above

28. The female hormone, estrogen, (ref. p. 39)
    a. is secreted by the anterior pituitary
    b. is associated with lactation
    c. is produced during the second half of the menstrual cycle
    d. leads to the development of secondary sex characteristics in the female

29. The male hormone, testosterone, (ref. p. 39)
    a. is secreted by the anterior pituitary
    b. brings about the primary sex characteristics in the male
    c. is produced by the interstitial cells of the testes
    d. all of the above

30. Hormone replacement therapy (HRT) may protect women against (ref. p. 40)
    a. breast cancer
    b. coronary artery disease
    c. dysmenorrhea
    d. all of the above

31. The genetic composition of a normal male child is (ref. p. 41)
    a. 46 chromosomes, two of which are sex chromosomes (XX)
    b. 46 chromosomes, two of which are sex chromosomes (XY)
    c. 23 chromosomes, two of which are sex chromosomes (XX)
    d. 23 chromosomes, two of which are sex chromosomes (XY)

32. Which of the following research methods are designed to investigate the relative importance of genetic and environmental factors that contribute to the development of medical disorders? (ref. p. 41)
    a. studies of identical twins and fraternal twins
    b. studies of identical twins reared apart
    c. studies of adopted children
    d. all of the above

33. Dan and Sue are 3-year-old twins who are almost indistinguishable when dressed in the matching outfits their parents usually purchase for them. Based on this information, one can safely conclude that Dan and Sue (ref. p. 41)
    a. are fraternal twins
    b. are identical twins
    c. share more of their genetic makeup than other brothers and sisters
    d. none of the above

34. The study of genetics is important to health psychologists because (ref. p. 42)
    a. all medical disorders ultimately have a genetic component
    b. individual susceptibility to certain diseases may be inherited
    c. genetically based disorders are associated with superior psychological functioning since families have learned to cope with medical problems
    d. all of the above

35. Prenatal diagnostic tests are currently available that permit the detection of (ref. p. 42)
    a. epilepsy
    b. breast and colon cancer
    c. Huntington's disease
    d. none of the above

36. The case of Helen, who is healthy but has infected others with the AIDS virus, is an example of (ref. pp. 42–43)
    a. direct transmission of disease
    b. indirect transmission of disease
    c. biological transmission of disease
    d. mechanical transmission of disease

37. Nonspecific immunity may be mediated by the (ref. p. 44)
    a. skin
    b. phagocytes
    c. inflammatory response
    d. all of the above

38. The course of infection follows a specific sequence; that is (ref. p. 44)
    a. incubation period, period of nonspecific symptoms, acute phase, period of decline
    b. period of nonspecific symptoms, incubation period, acute phase, period of decline
    c. acute phase, incubation period, period of nonspecific symptoms, period of decline
    d. incubation period, acute phase, period of decline

39. A localized infection (ref. p. 44)
    a. is confined to a particular site and does not spread
    b. is confined to a particular area and sends toxins to other parts of the body
    c. occurs when the body's resistance is lowered from fighting a primary infection
    d. none of the above

40. Humoral immunity is mediated by (ref. p. 45)
    a. B cells
    b. helper and suppressor T cells
    c. B cells and helper and suppressor T cells
    d. none of the above

41. The spleen (ref. p. 46)
    a. secretes insulin and bile into the bloodstream
    b. produces neurotransmitters and corticosteroids
    c. produces B and T cells and filters the blood
    d. is primarily a vestigial organ

42. Hodgkin's disease involves (ref. p. 47)
    a. an inflammation of the lymphatic vessels
    b. the progressive, chronic enlargement of tissues of the lymphatic system
    c. a viral disorder marked by a large number of monocytes
    d. none of the above

43. Autoimmunity (ref. p. 47)
    a. involves the progressive, chronic enlargement of lymphatic tissue
    b. is a viral disorder marked by an unusually large number of monocytes
    c. is acquired through measures such as vaccination
    d. is a condition in which a specific humoral or cell-mediated immune response attacks the body's own tissue

44.   Autoimmunity may be implicated in (ref. p. 47)
    a. certain allergic responses
    b. arthritis
    c. multiple sclerosis
    d. all of the above

45.   Which of the following is **not** a disorder of lifestyle? (ref. pp. 17-47)
    a. lung cancer
    b. atherosclerosis
    c. Type I diabetes
    d. arteriosclerosis

Essay Questions

1. Describe the functioning of the autonomic nervous system. Include in your answer the roles of the sympathetic and parasympathetic nervous system in response to stress. (ref. p. 21)

2. Explain how smoking and a high-fat diet are risk factors for coronary heart disease. (ref. pp. 27–29)

3. Describe the nature and symptomatology of hepatitis. Compare and contrast Hepatitis A and Hepatitis B, including discussion of etiology and mode of transmission. (ref. pp. 36–37)

4. Explain how a health psychologist might employ family studies and twin to study the genetic basis of a health disorder. (ref. p. 41)

5. Compare and contrast nonspecific and specific immune mechanisms. Provide at least two examples of each. (ref. pp. 44–45)

CHAPTER 3
HEALTH BEHAVIORS

Chapter Outline

I.   Health Promotion: An Overview

II.   An Introduction to Health Behaviors

      A.   Role of Behavioral Factors in Disease and Disorder

      B.   What Are Health Behaviors?

      C.   Practicing and Changing Health Habits: An Overview

      D.   Intervening with Children and Adolescents

      E.   Interventions with At-Risk People

      F.   Health Promotion and the Elderly

      G.   Ethnic and Gender Differences in Health Risks and Habits

III.   Changing Health Habits

      A.   Attitude Change and Health Behavior

            1.   Educational Appeals

            2.   Fear Appeals

      B.   The Health Belief Model

            1.   Self-Efficacy and Health Behaviors

      C.   Theory of Planned Behavior

IV.   Cognitive-Behavioral Approaches to Health Behavior Change

      A.   Self-Observation and Self-Monitoring

      B.   Classical Conditioning

      C.   Operant Conditioning

      D.   Modeling

      E.   Stimulus Control

      F.   The Self-Control of Behavior

            1.   Self-Reinforcement

Learning Objectives

1. Define health promotion and describe the factors that have fueled the movement toward health promotion in the United States.

2. Summarize trends in the changing pattern of disease in the United States since the turn of the century.

3. Define health behaviors, health habits, and primary prevention.

4. Describe health-habit factors that undermine health practices.

5. Summarize the relationship of individual difference variables, social factors, emotional factors, cognitive factors, perceived symptoms, and factors related to access to medical care to health behaviors.

6. Summarize the findings of research investigating the success of health promotion and primary prevention efforts across the lifespan and with at-risk people. Describe ethnic and gender differences in health behaviors.

7. Summarize the effectiveness of attitudinal approaches and the use of fear appeals in changing attitudes and health behaviors.

8. Describe the components of the health belief model and explain how useful it is in predicting and changing health behaviors.

9. Define self-efficacy and explain the relationship between self-efficacy and health behaviors.

10. Describe the components of the Theory of Planned Behavior and evaluate its usefulness in predicting health behaviors.

11. Describe the basic principles of cognitive-behavioral therapy.

12. Define self-observation and self-monitoring and describe their use in cognitive-behavioral therapy.

13. Define classical conditioning, unconditioned response, conditioned response, unconditioned stimulus, and conditioned stimulus. Describe the use of classical conditioning in cognitive-behavioral therapy.

14. Define operant conditioning and differentiate between different schedules of reinforcement. Describe the use of operant conditioning in cognitive-behavioral therapy.

15. Define modeling, and describe its use in cognitive-behavioral therapy.

16. Define discriminative stimulus. Describe the use of stimulus-control interventions in cognitive-behavioral therapy.

17. Define self-reinforcement, self-reward, and self-punishment. Describe the use of self-reinforcement in cognitive-behavioral therapy.

18. Define contingency contracting, and describe its use in cognitive-behavioral therapy.

19. Define covert self-control, cognitive restructuring, and self-talk. Describe the use of covert self-control in cognitive-behavior therapy.

20. Define behavioral assignments, and describe their use in cognitive-behavior therapy.

21. Define skills and relaxation training and describe their use in cognitive-behavioral therapy.

22. Describe the principles of broad-spectrum therapy. Summarize the advantages of a multimodal approach to health behavior change.

23. Explain the nature and rate of relapse in addictive disorders and health behavior change.

24. Explain the factors that are predictive of relapse.

25. Explain the abstinence violation effect and its relationship to relapse.

26. Describe behavioral interventions to control relapse and their effectiveness in relapse prevention.

27. Describe the stages of health behavior change and the effectiveness of this model in explaining health behavior change.

28. Describe the use of social engineering in changing health behaviors.

29. Describe the use of various venues for changing health behaviors, and summarize the advantages and disadvantages of each.

Lecture Suggestions

Conceptions of Health and Illness Across the Life Span

Children's understanding of health and illness is limited by their cognitive development. That is not to say, however, that children are unable to take responsibility for certain health-related behaviors. In fact, childhood may be a very important period during which health habits are established. Two recent reviews of the child health psychology literature (Burbach & Peterson, 1986; Maddux, Roberts, Sledden, & Wright, 1986) suggest that children can, and do, assume responsibility for their health behaviors as they mature. Bibace and Walsh (1979) present a six-stage Piagetian model of the development of children's conceptions of illness. In addition, Leventhal, Prohaska, and Hirschman (1985) review the research investigating age differences in older and younger adults' health behaviors and perceptions of vulnerability. Discussing these age differences in class would provide an opportunity for students to consider the stability of health habits within the changing social context with which older individuals are faced.

Bibace, R., & Walsh, M. E. (1979). Developmental stages in children's conceptions of illness. In G. C. Stone, F. Cohen, & N. E. Adler (Eds.), Health psychology, (pp. 285–302). San Francisco: Jossey-Bass.

Burbach, D. J., & Peterson, L. (1986). Children's concepts of physical illness: A review and critique of the cognitive-developmental literature. Health Psychology, 5, 307–325.

Leventhal, H., Prohaska, T. R., & Hirschman, R. S. (1985). Preventive health behavior across the life span. In J. C. Rosen & L. J. Solomon (Eds.), Prevention in health psychology. Hanover: University Press of New England.

Maddux, J. E., Roberts, M. C., Sledden, E. A., & Wright, L. (1986). Developmental issues in child health psychology. American Psychologist, 41, 25–34.

Health-Promotion Interventions: Children and the Elderly

The text's descriptions of lifestyle health-promotion programs can be developed by discussing interventions that target different age groups. Edited volumes by Wilson et al. (1997) and Weissberg, et al. (1997) describes a number of health promotion programs designed to improve children's health. The chapters describe a number of programs that have been developed for several venues (i.e., family, school, and community). Many chapters from these volumes also can be used to illustrate concepts from Chapters 4 and 5. As noted in the text, encouraging older adults to engage in exercise has been linked with decreased mortality (Paffenbarger et al., 1993), as well as increased strength (Butler, 1993) and slowing the age-related loss of lean body mass (McCartney et al., 1995).

Butler, R. N. (1993). Did you say 'sarcopenia'? Geriatrics, 48, 11–12.

McCartney, N., Hicks, A. L., Martin, J., & Webber, C. E. (1995). Long-term resistance training in the elderly: Effects on dynamic strength, exercise capacity, muscle, and bone. Journal of Gerontology: Biological Sciences, 50A, B97–B104.

Paffenbarger, R. S., Hyde, R. T., Wing, A. L., Lee, I., Jung, D. L., & Kampter, J. B. (1993). The association of changes in physical-activity level and other life-style characteristics with mortality among men. New England Journal of Medicine, 328, 538–545.

Weissberg, R. P., Gullotta, T. P., Hampton, R. L., Ryan, B. A., & Adams, G. R. (1997). (Eds.). Healthy children 2010: Enhancing children's wellness. Thousand Oaks, CA: Sage.

Wilson, D. K., Rodrigue, J. R., & Taylor, W. C. (1997). (Eds.) Health-promoting and health-compromising behaviors among minority adolescents. Washington, DC: American Psychological Association.

Exercises, Projects, and Activities

Health Locus of Control Scale

Have students complete the Health Locus of Control Scale in class. A discussion of students' scores on each of the subscales should make the multidimensional nature of the scale clear. Ask students if they feel that their scores would be predictive of their typical health habits. Students living on campus in residential colleges often underestimate the effect that dormitory and cafeteria schedules have on their health habits. Two versions of the complete scale, scoring instructions, and normative information are available in Wallston, Wallston, and DeVellis (1978).

Wallston, K. A., Wallston, B. S., & DeVellis, R. (1978). Development of the multidimensional health locus of control (MHLC) scales. Health Education Monographs, 6, 160–170.

Health Consciousness Scale

Stephen J. Gould describes a scale designed to assess self-focused attention to one's personal health. This scale may be distributed, completed, and scored in class. Gould presents evidence that scores on the scale's four factors (i.e., health self-consciousness, health alertness, health self-monitoring, and health involvement) are related to self-reported health-related variables. Ask students if they feel their scores reflect their self-perceived concern for their health and whether their scores would be predictive of their usual health behaviors. The complete scales, scoring instructions, and normative information are available in Gould (1990).

Gould, S. J. (1990). Health consciousness and health behavior: The application of a new health consciousness scale. American Journal of Preventive Medicine, 6, 228-237.

Analysis of Media Appeals

Have students bring to class two to three media appeals designed to modify health behaviors (e.g., a magazine advertisement from the American Cancer Society) and discuss the effectiveness of each appeal. The effectiveness of each appeal could be analyzed in terms of the text's discussion of factors influencing the effectiveness of health messages. The text notes that a number of factors often limit the effectiveness of such messages, and a discussion of specific media appeals may reinforce the importance of these factors.

Health Belief Model

An independent project would provide an opportunity for students to critically evaluate the relationship between beliefs and attitudes toward health promotion and wellness. Have students interview a friend about his or her health-related beliefs, attitudes, and behaviors and analyze them within the context of the issues discussed in Chapter 3 and lecture. Assignments might be structured in a manner similar to the sample assignment that follows:

1. Develop a brief interview format that you will use to discuss the relevant beliefs, attitudes, and behaviors. Make it specific in order to address the goals of this assignment. Include your interview format as an appendix to your assignment.

2. Discuss the specific responses in relationship to health promotion and wellness (e.g., eating habits, contraception, avoidance of health-compromising behaviors, etc.). For example, do any of these beliefs relate to components of the health belief model? Does your friend indicate that normative pressures influence his or her beliefs or attitudes?

3. Explicitly discuss the relationship between actual behaviors and attitudes and beliefs. Do you find a strong positive relationship between beliefs and attitudes, or are some beliefs at odds with others? How are beliefs and attitudes translated into behaviors?

4. What do you conclude about your friend's health-related beliefs, attitudes, and behaviors? What factors seem to be involved in a good-attitude behavior match (if observed)? Can you identify factors that seem to explain why you fail to find good attitude-behavior concordance?

Cognitive-Behavioral Modification

Have students work in groups of three to four in order to develop a comprehensive multimodal cognitive behavioral therapy. Case histories that describe hypothetical patients, their psychosocial characteristics, and a target behavior to be changed can be prepared before class or can be developed by each group. Having each group report the nature of the intervention that has been designed presents an opportunity to assess students' comprehension of the principles of cognitive-behavioral modification. The text asserts that the complementary nature of methods chosen for such programs is a critical variable associated with successful health behavior modification. Discussing the reasons each group presents for including each component in the therapeutic program should reinforce this point.

Recommended Reading

Cautela, J. R., & Kearney, A. J. (1986). The covert conditioning handbook. New York: Springer.

An advanced text for students interested in learning more about covert conditioning techniques. It describes covert conditioning procedures and problems and provides an application of covert conditioning techniques to a number of behaviors.

Langer, E. J. (1989). Mindfulness. Reading, MA: Addison-Wesley.

This popular book summarizes 20 years of social psychological research investigating the role of control and context in individual behavior. The author describes how nonconscious processing of information can hamper the formation of positive habits. One chapter is dedicated to the influence of mindful information processing on health.

Meichenbaum, D. (1977). <u>Cognitive-behavior modification: An integrative approach</u>. New York: Plenum Press.

A classic, easy-to-read text that clearly presents the principles of cognitive-behavior modification for a general audience.

Shumaker, S. A., Schron, E., Ockene, J., & McBee, W. L. (Eds.) (1998). <u>The Handbook of Health Behavior Change</u>. New York: Springer.

Theoretical and empirical approaches to health behavior change are reviewed in this text for advanced students or practitioners. General models of behavior change and relapse preventions are discussed in addition to problems in promoting life-style interventions in high-risk groups.

True-False Questions

1. T   <u>F</u>   Patterns of disease in the United States have remained relatively unchanged over the past 90 years. (ref. p. 63)

2. <u>T</u>   F   By the age of 11 or 12, most children have fairly stable health beliefs that resemble those of adults. (ref. p. 53)

3. <u>T</u>   F   Instilling good health habits and changing poor ones are the task of primary prevention. (ref. p. 66)

4. T   <u>F</u>   The concept of the window of vulnerability refers to the fact that certain times are better for teaching particular health practices than others. (ref. p. 57)

5. <u>T</u>   F   Individuals often do not perceive their at-risk status accurately and appropriately. (ref. p. 58)

6. <u>T</u>   F   Health message communicators are more persuasive if they are likable, similar to the audience, and familiar to the audience. (ref. p. 62)

7. T   <u>F</u>   Research has established a small to moderate relationship between self-efficacy and health behavior change and maintenance. (ref. p. 66)

8. <u>T</u>   F   An important assumption of cognitive-behavioral therapy is that covert processes (i.e., thoughts and images) follow the same laws of learning and reinforcement as do external, observable behaviors. (ref. p. 75)

9. T   <u>F</u>   Most people attempt to modify their health habits through contact with private therapists or physicians. (ref. p. 86)

10. T   <u>F</u>   Mass media appeals are effective in alerting people to health risks and subsequently modifying their behavior. (ref. p. 91)

Multiple-Choice Questions

1. Which of the following is **not** an example of the health promotion and wellness approach to medical care? (ref. p. 51)
    <u>a</u>. medical interventions designed to assess and correct disease states
    b. the practice of good health behaviors
    c. the avoidance of health-compromising behaviors
    d. medical interventions designed to enhance and maximize good health

2. Compared to Americans living at the turn of the century, contemporary Americans are more likely to die from (ref. p. 52)
    a. acute infectious disorders
    b. diseases that were contracted during an epidemic, such as influenza
    c. disorders related to lifestyle
    d. none of the above

3. Approximately 25% of all cancer deaths can be attributable to (ref. p. 52)
    a. smoking
    b. overweight
    c. excessive alcohol consumption
    d. poor diet

4. According to the text, changing health behaviors may be beneficial because it (ref. p. 65)
    a. may reduce the number of deaths due to diseases related to lifestyle
    b. may increase individual longevity and life expectancy
    c. may delay the onset of chronic disease and enhance quality of life
    d. all of the above

5. Health habits (ref. p. 53)
    a. are highly resistant to change because they are continually reinforced by specific positive outcomes
    b. are unrelated to health behaviors
    c. require access to the health care delivery system
    d. are often performed without conscious awareness

6. Researchers (Belloc & Breslow, 1972) who conducted a longitudinal study of the health habits practiced by the residents of Alameda County found that (ref. p. 53)
    a. the more good health habits people practiced, the better they felt, and mortality rates were lower for both men and women at the 9 1/2 year follow-up
    b. although people who practiced a greater number of good health habits felt better, there was no difference in mortality rates at the 9 1/2 year follow-up
    c. although people who practiced a greater number of good health habits felt better, mortality rates were lower for women, but not men, at the 9 1/2 year follow-up
    d. none of the above

7. According to the demographic factors discussed in the text, which of the following individuals is most likely to practice good health behaviors? (ref. p. 54)
    a. Joe, a 45-year-old high school dropout who works two jobs in order to support his family
    b. Dan, a 30-year-old high school graduate who works as a file clerk in a small insurance agency who expects to be married next month
    c. Bill, a divorced 50-year-old corporate attorney
    d. Sam, a 30-year-old assistant professor who has just celebrated his fifth wedding anniversary

8. Considering the relationship of chronological age to health behaviors, good health behaviors would be **least** likely to be observed during (ref. p. 54)
   a. early childhood
   b. adolescence and early adulthood
   c. early and middle adulthood
   d. middle and late adulthood

9. One aspect of health habits that makes them difficult to modify is (ref. p. 55)
   a. they develop slowly; thus the exact point for intervention is seldom clear
   b. they are interdependent; a change in one habit is often reflect in changes in others
   c. factors controlling health behavior are generally consistent across the life span
   d. all of the above

10. Health-related habits such as food choices, snacking, and dieting begin to be established during the time children are attending (ref. p. 57)
   a. preschool
   b. elementary school
   c. junior high school
   d. high school

11. Research suggests that most people's perceptions of their own health risks are (ref. p. 58)
   a. unrealistically optimistic
   b. unrealistically pessimistic
   c. insensitive to feedback
   d. generally accurate

12. You are designing a health-promotion program for a retirement community. According to the text, which of the following behaviors would be the most important to target in your intervention? (ref. p. 60)
   a. eliminating smoking
   b. developing a regular exercise program
   c. reducing alcohol consumption
   d. maintaining a healthy diet

13. A health message that urges smokers to cut down or stop smoking would be most persuasive if it included a (ref. p. 62)
   a. statistical summary of the number of smokers who die each year from lung cancer
   b. frightening photo of cancerous lung tissue
   c. brief but vivid case history of a smoker who had successfully kicked the habit
   d. sufficient amount of fear-arousing information

14. Julia is designing a public service message designed to encourage adults to engage in moderate exercise. The be most effective, her message should address (ref. p. 62)
   a. weight gain experienced by sedentary adults as they age
   b. decreased flexibility associated with lack of exercise
   c. positive mood and enhanced well-being associated with aerobic exercise
   d. all of the above

15. The health belief model states that the practice of a particular health behavior is a function of (ref. p. 64)

   a. an individual's beliefs that he or she, rather than powerful others or chance, is in control of his or her own health

   b. an individual's attitudes about a health behavior, subjective normative beliefs, and self-efficacy

   <u>c</u>. an individual's beliefs in a specific health threat and beliefs that a specific health behavior can reduce that threat

   d. perceived self-efficacy and perceived invulnerability

16. Researchers have found a strong positive relationship between self-efficacy and (ref. p. 66)

   a. initial health behavior change

   b. long-term maintenance of health behavior change

   c. preventive health measures

   <u>d</u>. all of the above

17. According to the theory of planned behavior, behavioral intentions are a function of (ref. p. 66)

   <u>a</u>. specific health attitudes, normative beliefs, and perceptions of control

   b. general health attitudes, normative beliefs, and perceptions of control

   c. specific health attitudes and normative beliefs

   d. perceptions of vulnerability, magnitude of health threat, and self-efficacy

18. The author of your text concludes that attitudinal approaches to health behavior change (ref. pp. 67–68)

   <u>a</u>. are useful in predicting when people will become motivated to change their health behavior and make use of the medical health care system

   b. effectively explain the maintenance of good health behavior habits over long periods of time

   c. discriminate between individuals who successfully modify their health behaviors and those who do not

   d. none of the above

19. Len has started a diary as a first step in a smoking cessation program. He has noticed that he always reaches for an after-dinner cigarette. In this analysis, his usual place at the head of the family dinner table is the (ref. pp. 68–69)

   <u>a</u>. antecedent

   b. consequent

   c. target behavior

   d. none of the above

20. The use of Antabuse in the treatment of alcoholism is an example of (ref. p. 69)

   a. shaping

   b. modeling

   c. operant conditioning

   <u>d</u>. classical conditioning

21. The use of Antabuse in the treatment of alcoholism involves having the client sip his or her favorite drink while ingesting Antabuse. After a number of pairings, alcohol becomes a(n) _____ which elicits a(n) _____. (ref. p. 69)
    a. conditioned response; conditioned stimulus
    b. conditioned stimulus; conditioned response
    c. unconditioned response; unconditioned stimulus
    d. unconditioned stimulus; unconditioned response

22. Classical conditioning modifies the _____ of behavior; operant conditioning modifies the _____ of behavior. (ref. pp. 69–70)
    a. consequents; consequents
    b. consequents; antecedents
    c. antecedents; consequents
    d. antecedents; antecedents

23. The use of rewards for weight loss (e.g., money or new clothing) in the treatment of obesity is an example of (ref. p. 71)
    a. shaping
    b. modeling
    c. operant conditioning
    d. classical conditioning

24. A behavioral response is most resistant to extinction if it is subject to a _____ schedule of reinforcement. (ref. p. 71)
    a. continuous
    b. variable
    c. random
    d. maintenance

25. The use of ex-addicts as peer counselors in drug treatment programs is an example of (ref. p. 71)
    a. shaping
    b. modeling
    c. operant conditioning
    d. classical conditioning

26. According to a study of children's fears of receiving inoculations conducted by Vernon (1974), (ref. p. 71)
    a. children who viewed a film that depicted models who briefly displayed moderate levels of pain and emotion experienced more distress than children who viewed a film that depicted fearless models
    b. children who viewed a film that depicted models who briefly displayed moderate levels of pain and emotion experienced less distress than children who viewed a film that depicted fearless models
    c. children who viewed a film that depicted same-sex models experienced less distress than children who viewed a film that depicted opposite-sex models
    d. the nature of the film did not have an effect; each film was equally effective in distracting the children

27. A discriminative stimulus (ref. p. 72)
    a. is a central component of therapies based on classical conditioning
    b. becomes reinforcing through pairing with the unconditioned stimulus
    c. serves as a cue that positively reinforcing responses or behavior will occur
    d. all of the above

28. Brenda has been trying to lose weight and control her seemingly insatiable sweet tooth. To meet her goal, she has removed all cookies, candy, and ice cream from the kitchen cabinets and refrigerator. She also has begun keeping a bowl of fresh fruit on the kitchen counter from which she may nibble freely. Brenda is practicing (ref. p. 72)
    a. vicarious self-control
    b. self-punishment
    c. stimulus control
    d. self-reinforcement

29. Self-punishment (ref. p. 73)
    a. is as effective in changing behavior as self-reward
    b. is most effective in changing behavior when it is also coupled with self-reward
    c. is effective in behavior change even when individuals stop performing the target behavior
    d. becomes increasingly effective as the punishment becomes increasingly aversive

30. Fred wants to lose twenty pounds. He places twenty one-pound boxes of lard in the refrigerator. As his weight-loss program proceeds, he removes one box of lard each time he succeeds in losing a pound. In this instance, Fred is using (ref. p. 74)
    a. positive self-punishment
    b. negative self-punishment
    c. positive self-reward
    d. negative self-reward

31. Rhonda entered into an agreement with her friend, Nancy, in an attempt to establish a regular exercise program. According to their agreement, Nancy pays Rhonda $1 every day that she exercises for at least 30 minutes after work. If she fails to do so, Rhonda must pay Nancy $1. This is an example of (ref. p. 74)
    a. shaping
    b. a token economy
    c. a contingency contract
    d. vicarious reinforcement

32. Internal monologues (ref. p. 74)
    a. are always positive and adaptive
    b. can act as reinforcements or punishments for other behaviors
    c. are resistant to change through standard techniques of reinforcement
    d. can function as antecedents but not consequents of target behavior

33. Wanda's weight-loss counselor has observed that she has a self-defeating pattern of beliefs and cognitions about her ability to control her overeating. Specifically, when she eats something that is not allowed on her diet she thinks "I have no willpower. I'll always be fat" and binges the rest of the day. Wanda's counselor now is encouraging her to think "Well, I slipped on my diet at lunch. Relax, one slip isn't that bad. I'll get back on my diet right away!" The therapist is utilizing a technique called (ref. p. 75)

   a. cognitive restructuring
   b. positive reinforcement
   c. self-monitoring
   d. self-punishment

34. Behavioral assignments (ref. pp. 75–76)

   a. place complete responsibility and control in the hands of the therapist who develops the assignments and thus decrease clients' perceptions of control
   b. show great promise but have not been extensively used in health management programs to date
   c. that rely upon written agreements are most effective because they facilitate behavioral analysis and treatment implementation
   d. that rely upon verbal agreements are most effective because their flexibility enhances clients' perceptions of control

35. Which of the following is **not** a goal of skills training? (ref. p. 76)

   a. reducing anxiety that is associated with social situations
   b. introducing new skills for dealing with anxiety-arousing situations
   c. providing alternatives for maladaptive behaviors
   d. none of the above

36. Relaxation training is an important component of systematic desensitization because it (ref. p. 76)

   a. distracts the client from the anxiety-provoking situation
   b. allows the therapist to "flood" the client with emotional images
   c. makes the use of an anxiety hierarchy unnecessary
   d. is a response that is substituted for anxiety

37. Relapse (ref. p. 79)

   a. is more likely to be observed in instances of declining motivation and lack of goals
   b. appears to be unrelated to situational factors; it is almost exclusively an individual problem
   c. has been found to have similar rates and patterns for alcohol and drug addiction, but relapse rates for smokers increase with the passage of time
   d. is unrelated to levels of perceived stress and social support

38. An abstinence violation effect is associated with (ref. p. 79)

   a. psychological reactance and an increased feeling of perceived control
   b. an increased feeling of perceived control and decreased likelihood of relapse
   c. a loss of perceived control and increased likelihood of relapse
   d. none of the above

39. Schachter (1982) has argued that (ref. p. 80)
   a. relapse rates are usually overestimated
   b. smokers often successfully quit after repeated attempts
   c. booster sessions are useful in preventing relapse
   d. relapse leads to learned helplessness and decreased perceptions of control

40. Relapse prevention techniques often adopt cue exposure techniques which (ref. pp. 81–82)
   a. extinguish the craving typically evoked by a cue, such as an alcoholic beverage
   b. increase feelings of self-efficacy
   c. reduce positive expectations associated with the addictive behavior
   d. all of the above

41. Julian has decided that he needs to lose 15 pounds. He is concerned about the amount of fat he consumes, and suspects that his cholesterol count is high. He has purchased a popular book on low-fat diets, and has decided that he will begin walking three times a week after he buys a new pair of walking shoes next week. According to Prochaska et al.'s (1992) transtheoretical model of behavioral change, Julian is in the _____ stage of health behavior change. (ref. pp. 82–83)
   a. precontemplation
   b. contemplation
   c. preparation
   d. action

42. Studies evaluating the effectiveness of Prochaska et al.'s (1992) transtheoretical model of behavioral change indicate that (ref. p. 84)
   a. interventions matched to the stage that an individual is in are more successful than those more appropriate for other stages
   b. interventions that teach skills relevant to action and behavior maintenance have little effect upon individual motivation
   c. the media have even less of an effect upon an individual's health behaviors than previously thought
   d. it has little predictive utility

43. Self-help groups (ref. p. 85)
   a. are a primary means of health-habit modification in this country
   b. are an ineffective means of health-habit modification; most Americans prefer to visit a private therapist or physician
   c. provide valuable social support to their members, but seldom employ cognitive-behavioral methods
   d. none of the above

44. The family physician may be a particularly effective agent in the promotion of health-related attitudes and behavior because (ref. p. 86)
   a. individuals are more likely to follow a suggested treatment if they pay for professional advice
   b. few social engineering solutions to health problems have been successful
   c. a one-to-one approach is the least expensive and most efficient vehicle for changing health habits
   d. a physician is a highly credible communicator and agent of health-habit change

45. Evaluations of the efficacy of mass media health appeals suggest that (ref. p. 90)
    a. messages are often too concrete and specific and thus it is difficult to glean useful information from mass media appeals
    b. including specific recommendations about health-related behaviors diminishes individual perceptions of self-efficacy
    c. mass media messages are unrelated to shifts in cultural climate
    d. media appeals are often important sources of information for alerting the public to unknown health risks

Essay Questions

1. How have patterns of disease in the United States changed since the turn of the century? Considering these trends, explain the importance of efforts to modify health behaviors and life-style rebalancing. (ref. pp. 53–56)

2. Explain the advantages and disadvantages of health promotion efforts designed for at-risk populations. (ref. pp. 58–59)

3. How effective are educational appeals designed to provide information about health, risk factors and wellness? What aspects of educational appeals heighten their effectiveness? What aspects make them less effective in changing attitudes and behaviors? (ref. pp. 62–63)

4. Charles is a college student who smokes cigarettes. Use the health belief model and the theory of planned behavior to explain why Charles continues to smoke even though he is aware of the Surgeon General's warning about the relationship between cigarettes and cancer and heart disease. (ref. pp. 64–68)

5. Describe the problem of relapse. Explain how relapse prevention might be incorporated in broad-spectrum cognitive-behavior therapy treatment plan for (choose one) alcoholism, smoking, or obesity. Be sure to include in your answer specific cognitive-behavior techniques and their role in the therapeutic plan. (ref. pp. 68–82)

CHAPTER 4
HEALTH-ENHANCING BEHAVIORS

Chapter Outline

I.   Exercise

    A.   Benefits of Exercise

    B.   Determinants of Regular Exercise

        1.   Individual Characteristics

        2.   Characteristics of the Setting

        3.   Characteristics of Intervention Strategies

II.   Accident Prevention

    A.   Home and Workplace Accidents

    B.   Motorcycle and Automobile Accidents

III. Cancer-Related Health Behaviors

    A.   Breast Self-Examination

    B.   Mammography

    C.   Testicular Self-Examination

    D.   Sunscreen Use

IV.   Weight Control

    A.   The Regulation of Eating

    B.   Why Obesity Is a Health Risk

    C.   Factors Associated with Obesity

    D.   Stress and Eating

    E.   Treatment of Obesity

        1.   Dieting

        2.   Fasting

        3.   Surgery

4. Appetite-Suppressing Drugs

5. Behavior Modification

6. The Multimodal Approach

7. Work Site Weight-Loss Interventions

8. Commercial Weight-Loss Programs

F. Evaluation of Cognitive-Behavioral Weight-Loss Techniques

G. Eating Disorders

1. Anorexia Nervosa

2. Bulimia

V. Diet

A. Postscript

Learning Objectives

1. Define aerobic exercise and contrast with isokinetic exercise.

2. Summarize the benefits of aerobic exercise.

3. Describe the typical aerobic exercise prescription.

4. Summarize the individual characteristics associated with adherence to exercise regimens.

5. Summarize the characteristics of the setting associated with adherence to exercise regimens.

6. Summarize the characteristics of intervention associated with adherence to exercise regimens.

7. Describe the role of accidents as a major cause of death and injury in adults and children.

8. Describe the role of motorcycle and automobile accidents as a major cause of death and describe the effectiveness of strategies designed to increase seat belt usage and safety-related behavior.

9. Describe the process of breast self-examination and the factors that affect whether or not a woman will practice breast self-examination.

10. Describe strategies designed to increase the frequency of breast self-examination and their effectiveness.

11. Describe the nature of breast cancer and the role of mammography in detecting cancer.

12. Describe the problem of adherence to mammography recommendations and strategies for increasing women's use of mammography.

13. Describe the nature of testicular cancer, the role of testicular self-examination in detecting cancer, and the effectiveness of strategies designed to increase the frequency of testicular self-examination.

14. Describe the nature of skin cancer and strategies designed to increase the use of sunscreen.

15. Describe the physiological mechanisms involved in the regulation of eating.

16. Define obesity and explain why it is a health risk.

17. Describe the factors associated with obesity and the relationship between stress and eating.

18. Describe the nature of the treatment of obesity in the United States.

19. Explain the use of dieting, fasting, surgical procedures and appetite-suppressant drugs in treating obesity. Evaluate the effectiveness of each technique.

20. Explain the use of behavior modification in the treatment of obesity and evaluate its effectiveness.

21. Explain the use of the multimodal approach in treating obesity and evaluate its effectiveness.

22. Describe the nature of worksite weight-loss interventions and evaluate their effectiveness.

23. Describe the nature of commercial weight-loss programs and evaluate their effectiveness.

24. Summarize the effectiveness of cognitive-behavioral weight-loss techniques.

25. Explain the prevalence of eating disorders in Western countries.

26. Define anorexia nervosa, explain factors implicated in its development, and describe approaches to its treatment.

27. Define bulimia, explain factors implicated in its development, and describe approaches to its treatment.

28. Explain the health risks associated with a poor diet and describe the nature and effectiveness of dietary intervention programs.

Lecture Suggestions

Social Norms and Eating Behavior

The topic of eating disorders provides an opportunity to review the Theory of Planned Behavior and the influence of modeling and subjective norms on health-related behaviors. Crandall (1988) presented an analysis of normative pressures that were found to encourage binge eating in college students. Two campus sororities were identified which had evolved different norms about binge eating. In one group, a member's popularity was positively related to the amount of her binging. In the other group, the popular members were those who binged the "right amount." Finally, substantial social pressures to binge were evidenced in each group.

Crandall, C. S. (1988). Social contagion of binge eating. <u>Journal of Personality and Social Psychology, 55</u>, 588–598.

Self-Awareness and Bulimia

As the text notes, body image and other aspects of the self-concept are implicated in eating disorders. The role of the self in the development of eating disorders may be discussed in light of two recent theoretical models. Heatherton and Baumeister (1991) assert that binging is associated with a desire to reduce self-awareness. Because bulimics exhibit perfectionism and unrealistically high standards, the sensate focus afforded by binging reduces the aversive focus upon one's failure to meet these standards. In a similar light, Forston and Stanton (1992) argue that discrepancies in the actual versus ideal self are associated with bulimic symptomatology. They conclude that incompatible self-referent cognitions are more likely to be found among women with eating disorders.

Forston, M. T., & Stanton, A. L. (1992). Self-discrepancy theory as a framework for understanding bulimic symptomatology and associated distress. <u>Journal of Social and Clinical Psychology, 11</u>, 103–118.

Heatherton, T. F., & Baumeister, R. F. (1991). Binge eating as escape from self-awareness. <u>Psychological Bulletin, 110</u>, 86–108.

Exercises, Projects, and Activities

Personal Health Behavior Change

Assign an independent project and have students identify a health behavior of their own that they would like to modify. Complete projects might include a self-observation log that chronicles the behavioral antecedents, the target behavior, and its consequents; a planned cognitive-behavioral modification program designed to modify the behavior; and an evaluation of the effectiveness of the intervention.

Health Promotion and Wellness

One way to begin a discussion of health-enhancing behaviors would be to have students reflect on their personal practice of wellness. A number of lifestyle assessment measures are available that would provide a starting point for class discussion. One measure, the Healthstyle Inventory, is available by mail (Health Information Clearinghouse, P.O. Box 1133, Washington, DC 20013). A popular wellness text (Clark, 1981) contains a fairly lengthy personal habits questionnaire (How Well Am I?), which is designed to assess the frequency of health-related behaviors in six domains (diet, fitness, "feeling good," caring for self and others, fitting in, being responsible).

Clark, C. C. (1981). <u>Enhancing wellness</u>. New York: Springer.

Recommended Reading

Capaldi, E. D. (Ed.) (1996). <u>Why we eat what we eat: The psychology of eating</u>. Washington, DC: American Psychological Association.

Whereas the primary focus of this book is how people learn (and change) food preferences, chapters also discuss developmental, social, cognitive and physiological perspectives on normal hunger and eating. This volume presents a current and thorough review of the psychological research in this area.

Logue, A. W. (1991). <u>The psychology of eating and drinking</u> (2nd ed.). New York: W. H. Freeman.

This text presents a review of the biological, psychological, and social factors affecting hunger and thirst. Chapters address the physiological, genetic, and environmental determinants of hunger and thirst, eating and drinking disorders, and weight control.

Mahoney, M. J., & Mahoney, K. (1976). <u>Permanent weight control</u>. New York: Norton.

This is a self-help book written for a general audience. The authors describe the steps in developing and implementing a weight-control program based on the principles of cognitive-behavior modification.

Polivy, J., & Herman, C. P. (1983). <u>Breaking the diet habit: The natural weight alternative</u>. New York: Basic Books.

This volume summarizes the results of studies of restrained eating. The authors discuss the impact of dieting culture, obsessive behavior, and bizarre standards of physical attractiveness on eating behaviors. Bulimia and anorexia are also discussed.

Thompson, J. K. (Ed.) (1996). Body image, eating disorders and obesity: An integrative guide to assessment and treatment. Washington, DC: American Psychological Association.

This book presents an overview of body image and its relationship to anorexia nervosa, bulimia, binge eating, and obesity. The primary audience for this book is mental and health care personnel. Many chapters will be of interest to persons interested in health psychology, however, including etiology, diagnosis, treatment, and many case histories.

True-False Questions

1. <u>T</u>   F   People who engage in regular vigorous exercise may reduce their risk of certain forms of cancer. (ref. p. 95)

2. T   <u>F</u>   Because of social factors that encourage weight-related concerns, girls and women of all ages engage in more exercise than do boys and men. (ref. p. 98)

3. <u>T</u>   F   People who drop out of exercise programs do so within the first 3 to 6 months. (ref. p. 99)

4. <u>T</u>   F   Compared to health education interventions, seat belt use is highest in areas where it is mandated by law. (ref. p. 102)

5. T   <u>F</u>   The majority of cancerous lumps are detected through mammography. (ref. p. 103)

6. <u>T</u>   <u>F</u>   Yo-yo dieting is more likely to produce changes in abdominal fat compared to fat in other parts of the body. (ref. p. 109)

7. <u>T</u>   F   Compared to interventions with adults, cognitive-behavioral weight-loss programs appear to be more successful in treating childhood obesity. (ref. p. 119)

8. T   <u>F</u>   Body image distortions have been found to cause anorexia. (ref. p. 122)

9. <u>T</u>   F   Reducing dietary cholesterol is associated with decreased risk of CHD. (ref. p. 125)

10. <u>T</u>   F   Low cholesterol diets contribute to negative mood and behavior problems. (ref. p. 126)

Multiple-Choice Questions

1. Aerobic exercise involves _____ activities. (ref. p. 95)
   a. low-intensity, long-duration
   b. low-intensity, short-duration
   <u>c.</u> high-intensity, long-duration
   d. high-intensity, short-duration

2. Isokinetic exercise involves _____ activities. (ref. p. 95)
   a. low-intensity, long-duration
   b. low-intensity, short-duration
   c. high-intensity, long-duration
   <u>d.</u> high-intensity, short-duration

3. Which of the following is <u>not</u> one of the established benefits of aerobic exercise? (ref. p. 95)
   a. control of hypertension
   <u>b.</u> improved attention and concentration
   c. improved cardiovascular functioning
   d. reductions in poor health habits

4. The typical aerobic exercise prescription is performing at _____ of maximal heart rate nonstop for a minimum of _____ , three times per week. (ref. p. 95)
   a. 50% to 75%; 15 minutes
   b. 50% to 75%; 30 minutes
   <u>c.</u> 70% to 85%; 15 minutes
   d. 70% to 85%; 30 minutes

5. The physiological response to exercise and stress is similar (i.e., the release of adrenaline and other hormones). The beneficial effect of exercise on heart functioning may be due to the fact that (ref. p. 96)
   a. infrequent activation and discharge of adrenaline may be beneficial
   b. adrenaline released in response to stress may be metabolized differently than that released during exercise
   c. hypothalamic-pituitary-adrenocorticol (HPA) axis activation under conditions of stress heightens the harmful effects of sympathetic nervous system activity
   <u>d.</u> all of the above

6. Researchers investigating the effect of aerobic exercise on psychological functioning conclude that (ref. pp. 95–96)

   a. exercise appears to have a modest effect on mood and well-being immediately following a workout

   b. whereas immediate improvements in mood and well-being are associated with aerobic exercise, long-term participation in an exercise program has an even stronger effect on mood and mental health

   c. the positive effect of exercise on mood is unrelated to increased self-efficacy

   d. whereas exercise is associated with improved mood, it has no effect on personality variables such as the self-concept and self-esteem

7. Exercise (ref. p. 97)

   a. has been consistently associated with improved attention and concentration

   b. has been consistently associated with improved attention but not concentration

   c. may initially facilitate attention but this gain may be canceled out by the effects of fatigue

   d. has not been found to have any effect on cognitive processes

8. Aerobic exercise is said to buffer the effects of stress. This assertion is supported by research which has found that (ref. p. 97)

   a. employee fitness programs reduce absenteeism, increase job satisfaction, and reduce health care costs, especially among males

   b. the negative impact of stressful life events is positively correlated with exercise levels

   c. exercise appears to suppress the immune system

   d. exercise appears to modulate immune activity during stress

9. The average dropout rate reported in studies of adherence to exercise regimens is approximately _____ by the end of the first 6 months. (ref. p. 97)

   a. 30%

   b. 50%

   c. 70%

   d. 85%

10. Which of the following people are **least** likely to exercise regularly? (ref. p. 98)

   a. Joe, a 10-year old boy

   b. Jill, a 15-year-old girl

   c. Jack, a 35-year-old man

   d. Juana, a 45-year-old woman

11. Self-efficacy has been found to be related to positive affect derived from exercise in that (ref. p. 98)

   a. subjects with high self-efficacy beliefs reported more positive affect

   b. positive affect has been found to predict subsequent self-efficacy beliefs

   c. subjects with low self-efficacy beliefs are less likely to exercise

   d. all of the above

12. Of the following, the best predictor of long-term adherence to an exercise regimen is (ref. p. 99)
    a. positive attitudes toward exercise and health
    b. the belief that people should take responsibility for their health
    c. general health status
    d. convenient and easily accessible opportunities for exercise

13. Studies of intervention strategies to promote regular exercise have found (ref. pp. 99–100)
    a. exercise interventions may generalize to other lifestyle changes
    b. relapse is less frequent among subjects who attempt novel and challenging activities
    c. the exercise level in the American population is still declining at an alarming rate
    d. all of the above

14. The single greatest cause of accidental death is (ref. p. 100)
    a. motorcycle and automobile accidents
    b. accidental poisoning or falls
    c. occupational accidents
    d. household accidents

15. The increase in child safety-related behaviors appears to be attributable to (ref. pp. 100–101)
    a. social engineering requiring the use of safety restraints
    b. mass media interventions and parental education
    c. increased availability and use of car seats
    d. all of the above

16. The practice of breast self-examination (BSE) has been found to be predicted by (ref. p. 103)
    a. general concern for physical fitness
    b. favorable attitudes toward breast self-examination
    c. fear of breast cancer
    d. all of the above

17. Failing to engage in regular breast self-examinations (BSE) is associated with (ref. p. 103)
    a. lack of knowledge about practicing BSE effectively
    b. difficulty in detecting lumps
    c. difficulty in remembering the monthly schedule
    d. all of the above

18. Which of the following is the most effective method to teach women to correctly practice breast-self examination? (ref. p. 103)
    a. personal instruction by a physician or other medical personnel
    b. personal instruction by a physician or other medical personnel using a live or synthetic model
    c. printed instructions (e.g., pamphlets)
    d. printed instructions (e.g., pamphlets) and mail prompts

19. Which of the following is <u>not</u> a factor that reduces compliance with mammography recommendations? (ref. p. 105)
    <u>a</u>. Early detection of breast cancer through the use of mammography has had little effect upon survival rates.
    b. Mammograms frequently are not a standard part of older women's medical care.
    c. Older women have fragmented medical care.
    d. Minority women often do not have a regular source of health care.

20. Breast cancer and testicular cancer are similar in that (ref. p. 106)
    a. the average age of onset is increasing
    b. both are a common cause of death in young adults
    c. the likelihood of survival is high
    <u>d</u>. the likelihood of survival improves with early detection

21. The Theory of Planned Behavior has been found to predict regular (ref. pp. 102–107)
    a. sunscreen use
    <u>b</u>. breast self-exams (BSE)
    c. seat belt use
    d. all of the above

22. The _____ controls eating through the release of gastrointestinal and pancreatic hormones. The _____ controls eating through a concentration of neuropeptides and other neurotransmitters. (ref. p. 107)
    a. central feeding mechanism; central satiety system
    b. peripheral feeding mechanism; peripheral satiety system
    <u>c</u>. peripheral satiety system; central feeding mechanism
    d. central satiety system; peripheral feeding mechanism

23. Obesity is defined as being in excess of _____ one's ideal body weight. (ref. p. 107)
    a. 10%
    b. 15%
    <u>c</u>. 20%
    d. 30%

24. Recent epidemiological evidence suggests that fat in the _____ is an especially potent risk factor for disease. (ref. p. 108)
    <u>a</u>. abdomen
    b. hips and buttocks
    c. abdomen, hips, and buttocks
    d. none of the above

25. Overeating in adolescence and adulthood is likely to affect (ref. p. 109)
    <u>a</u>. the size of fat cells
    b. the number of fat cells
    c. both the size and number of fat cells
    d. the metabolic rate

26. People who gain and lose weight in cycles (yo-yo dieters) increase their chances for becoming obese because they (ref. p. 111)
   a. develop more poor health habits with each diet cycle
   b. increase their number of fat cells with each diet cycle
   c. decrease their metabolic rate with each diet cycle
   d. decrease their motivation with each diet cycle

27. According to Brownell and Wadden (1992), each individual has an ideal biological weight that is resistant to modification. This ideal biological weight is one's (ref. p. 111)
   a. metabolic rate
   b. set point
   c. internal point
   d. cultural ideal

28. According to Rodin and her associates (1989), _____ may be predisposing factors for obesity. (ref. p. 112)
   a. negative affect, externality, and lack of impulse control
   b. dependency and negative affect
   c. depression and anxiety
   d. none of the above

29. People's eating behavior often responds to stress, in that (ref. p. 112–114)
   a. men eat more when they are stressed
   b. stress influences the type of food women and men consume
   c. reactivity to stress appears to be a function of obesity rather than dieting, per se
   d. none of the above

30. Currently, the most common approach to the control of obesity is (ref. p. 114–117)
   a. fasting or dieting
   b. behavioral modification
   c. fasting or dieting and behavioral modification
   d. surgical interventions

31. Dieting (ref. pp. 114–115)
   a. is a slow, but eventually effective, treatment for obesity
   b. produces small, short-term weight losses
   c. has physiological, but not psychological, effects
   d. none of the above

32. Several studies now show that consumption of _____ prior to a meal reduces caloric and fat intake. (ref. p. 117)
   a. water
   b. glucose
   c. fructose
   d. any of the above

33. Analyses of the University of Pennsylvania's multimodal program to modify obesity have prompted further program development. The new program has incorporated (ref. p. 118)

   a. exercise

   b. cognitive restructuring

   c. social support

   <u>d</u>. all of the above

34. Evaluations of cognitive-behavioral weight-loss programs conclude that (ref. p. 119)

   a. such programs are unlikely to meet most people's needs as 95% of all diets fail

   b. such programs produce only modest weight loss and maintenance of weight loss

   <u>c</u>. longer programs that include exercise and relapse prevention are most successful

   d. such programs appear to be more useful for severely obese persons than for mildly obese persons

35. Which of the following is **not** an argument supporting the use of a prevention model to obesity? (ref. p. 119)

   a. Individual responses to cognitive-behavioral treatment are highly variable.

   <u>b</u>. Problems with self-control are less likely to be found among children.

   c. Trends indicate that the prevalence of obesity in the United States is increasing.

   d. Age-related weight gain among normal-weight adults can be prevented with life-style interventions.

36. Anorexia nervosa is (ref. p. 121)

   a. caused by amenorrhea

   b. characterized by the binge-and-purge syndrome

   c. characterized by reduced interest in food and restricted physical activity

   <u>d</u>. characterized by dieting and exercising that results in weight loss that is significantly below optimal levels

37. Anorexia has been found to be correlated with (ref. p. 122)

   a. body image disturbance

   b. lack of control and high need for approval

   c. family dynamics

   <u>d</u>. all of the above

38. Mothers of daughters who exhibit eating disorders are (ref. p. 123)

   <u>a</u>. more vulnerable to eating disorders themselves

   b. more dissatisfied with their own appearance

   c. less dissatisfied with family functioning

   d. all of the above

39. Bulimics differ from anorectics in that (ref. p. 124)

   <u>a</u>. by definition anorectics are underweight; bulimics are often of normal weight or overweight

   b. bulimia is more commonly observed between the ages of 30 to 45

   c. anorexia is associated with diminished perceptions of control; bulimia is not

   d. anorexia may be associated with certain physiological factors; bulimia is associated with certain psychological factors

40. According to Polivy, Herman, and Olmstead (1984), a history of being overweight may be an important predictor of bulimia because (ref. p. 124)

    a. depression and anxiety are associated with being overweight

    b. overweight individuals are more likely to have poor impulse control

    c. overweight individuals, as restrained eaters, may be more likely to binge

    d. none of the above

41. Bulimia is correlated with (ref. p. 124)

    a. stress and interpersonal conflict

    b. amenorrhea

    c. perfectionism

    d all of the above

42. Most therapies for anorexia utilize _____, whereas _____ appears to be the most effective treatment for bulimia. (ref. pp. 124–125)

    a. behavioral therapy; medication and cognitive-behavioral therapy

    b. medication; behavioral therapy

    c. medication and cognitive-behavioral therapy; inpatient treatment

    d. medication and inpatient treatment; cognitive-behavioral therapy

43. Poor diet has been linked with the incidence of (ref. p. 125)

    a. cancer

    b. coronary heart disease

    c. cardiovascular disease

    d. all of the above

44. Health experts urge a reduction in blood level cholesterol for those with a total count over (ref. p. 126)

    a. 500

    b. 300

    c. 200

    d. 100

45. Low-cholesterol diets have been linked to (ref. p. 126)

    a. reduced risk of coronary heart disease

    b. negative mood

    c. behavior problems

    d. all of the above

Essay Questions

1. Explain why exercise is so good for you. Include in your answer the physical and psychological outcomes associated with exercise. (ref. pp. 95–97)

2. As the text notes, people who are high in self-efficacy are more likely to adhere to exercise and weight-loss regimens. Summarize the research investigating the relationship between self-efficacy, exercise, obesity, and weight-loss. (ref. pp. 96–101; 109–118)

3. Suppose you are designing a program to be administered through the county health department designed to increase the frequency of breast self-examination (BSE) among community residents. Considering the research reviewed in the text, what techniques would be most effective to include in this program, and why? (ref. pp. 103–106)

4. Obesity tends to run in families. Citing the research from the text, explain why this is so. (ref. pp. 109–112)

5. Explain why recommendations to reduce cholesterol are controversial. Include in your answer an explanation of the advantages and disadvantages of adopting a low-cholesterol diet. (ref. pp. 125–129)

CHAPTER 5
HEALTH-COMPROMISING BEHAVIORS

Chapter Outline

1.   Nicotine Replacement Therapy

2.   Aversion Therapy

3.   Operant Conditioning

4.   Multimodal Intervention

     C.   Evaluation of Multimodal Interventions

     D.   Who Is Best Able to Induce People to Stop Smoking?

     E.   Why Is Smoking So Hard to Change?

     F.   People Who Stop on Their Own

V.   Smoking Prevention

     A.   Advantages of Smoking Prevention Programs

     B.   Social Influence Interventions

     C.   The Life-Skills Training Approach

     D.   Social Engineering and Smoking

Learning Objectives

1. Define health-compromising behaviors.

2. Explain the role of physical dependence and withdrawal in addiction.

3. Define alcoholism and problem drinking, and describe the prevalence and costs of alcohol abuse in the United States.

4. Describe the origins of alcoholism and problem drinking.

5. Describe the goals and nature of treatment programs for alcoholism and problem drinking.

6. Describe the use of behavior-modification, aversion therapy, and multimodal or broad-spectrum approaches in the treatment of alcoholism and problem drinking.

7. Describe the problem of relapse and the use of extinction training in reducing craving.

8. Summarize the factors associated with favorable treatment outcomes and the effectiveness of treatment programs.

9. Describe the controversy over whether recovered alcoholics may drink again and describe treatment programs that focus on controlled drinking skills.

10. Summarize the effectiveness of preventive approaches to alcohol abuse.

11. Describe the nature and prevalence of drunken driving.

12. Describe the relationship between moderate alcohol intake and coronary heart disease.

13. Describe the prevalence and costs of smoking in the United States.

14. Describe the synergistic effects of smoking.

15. Trace social trends in smoking in the United States.

16. Describe the physiological, psychological, and social factors that determine smoking in adolescents and adults.

17. Explain the nature of addiction in smoking.

18. Compare and contrast the nicotine fixed-effect theory, the nicotine regulation theory, the multiple regulation model, and Pomerleau and Pomerleau's theory.

19. Summarize the effectiveness of attitude-change campaigns to reduce smoking.

20. Describe the use of nicotine replacement therapy, aversion therapy, operant conditioning, and multimodal intervention in smoking cessation and evaluate the effectiveness of each.

21. Compare and contrast the effectiveness of different change agents in smoking cessation.

22. Explain why smoking is so difficult to change, the relationship between smoking and weight gain, and the nature of withdrawal.

23. Describe the variables characteristic of people who stop smoking on their own.

24. Describe the nature and advantages of smoking prevention programs.

25. Explain the use of social influence interventions in smoking cessation and evaluate their effectiveness.

26. Describe the life-skills training approach to smoking cessation and evaluate its effectiveness.

27. Describe the use of social engineering strategies in smoking cessation and evaluate their effectiveness.

Lecture Suggestions

Smokeless Tobacco Users

Media attention has been directed recently to the use of smokeless tobacco, especially by adolescents. The use of smokeless tobacco appears to comprise one component of a substance use cluster, and it is often associated with peer use and parental tolerance. Avry and his colleagues (1989) report the results of in-depth interviews with male adolescent users and their fathers. Results indicated that the use of smokeless tobacco was heavily influenced by social factors. Further, users appeared to have used other substances (particularly alcohol and marijuana) and reported having tried unsuccessfully to quit.

Avry, D. V., Lichtenstein, E., Severson, H., Weissman, W., & Seeley, J. R. (1989). An in-depth analysis of male adolescent smokeless tobacco users: Interviews with users and their fathers. Journal of Behavioral Medicine, 12, 449–467.

Preventing HIV Infection

Recently, health psychologists have investigated predictors of unsafe and safer sex among heterosexual men and women. These studies may be used to complement the text's presentation of health-compromising behaviors. For example, perceived susceptibility and barriers predicted subjects' willingness to engage in HIV-preventive behaviors (Yep, 1993) and while self-efficacy has been found to mediate condom use among college students, most did not perceive themselves to be at risk of HIV infection (Wulfert & Wan, 1993). Finally, women report that fear of negative reactions from others heavily influences attitudes toward carrying condoms (Wilson, Jaccard, Endias, & Minkoff, 1993).

Wilson, T. E., Jaccard, J., Endias, R., & Minkoff, H. (1993). Reducing the risk of HIV infection for women: An attitudinal analysis of condom-carrying behavior. Journal of Applied Social Psychology, 23, 1093–1110.

Wulfert, E., & Wan, C. K. (1993). Condom use: A self-efficacy model. Health Psychology, 12, 346–353.

Yep, G. A. (1993). Health beliefs and HIV prevention: Do they predict monogamy and condom use? Journal of Social Behavior and Personality, 8, 507–520.

Condom Use: An Application of the Transtheoretical Model of Change

The topic of condom use to prevent the transmission of sexually transmitted disease can be used to expand the text of health-compromising behaviors while also reviewing Prochaska's model. Grimley and colleagues (1997) critique intervention programs designed to reduce unsafe sexual behavior and describe an intervention program designed to move target populations through stages, from "never" to "always" using condoms.

Grimley, D. M., Prochaska, G. E., & Prochaska, J. O. (1997). Condom use adoption and continuation: A transtheoretical approach. Health Education Research, 12, 61–75.

Exercises, Projects, and Activities

Substance Abuse Programs

Assign groups of three to four students each the task of contacting community programs that target drug, alcohol, or other substance abuse. An increasing number of education and intervention programs that target school-aged children have been established, and many will be happy to provide educational materials that can form the basis of a discussion of the efficacy of such programs. Since many programs have a speaker board, an in-class presentation also might be effective in promoting discussion of different health-compromising behaviors.

The Surgeon General and Consumer Warnings

Ask students to bring to class advertisements for alcohol and cigarettes that carry a health warning from the Surgeon General. The message on these ads often is varied in an attempt to heighten the message's impact. An in-class discussion might focus on the use of the mass media in eliminating health-compromising behaviors, the health beliefs each message targets, how or why people may discount or fail to recall such messages, etc. The ethics and success of social engineering might also be introduced, especially if state or local laws have recently been proposed or enacted (e.g., smoking prohibitions on some airline flights).

Recommended Reading

Gatchel, R. J., Baum, A., & Singer, J. E. (Eds.). (1982). Handbook of psychology and health (Vol. I): Clinical psychology and behavioral medicine: Overlapping disciplines. Hillsdale: Erlbaum.

This volume provides an overview of the field of behavioral medicine that is most suitable for advanced students. A number of chapters review the literature in the areas of appetitive behaviors and addictive disorders.

Weissberg, R. P., Gullotta, T. P., Hampton, R. L., Ryan, B. A., & Adams, G. R. (Eds.) (1997). Healthy children 2010: Enhancing children's wellness. Thousand Oaks, CA: Sage.

Many of the chapters in this edited volume address family, school, and community prevention programs targeting children's mental and physical health. The co-occurrence of problem behaviors are described as well as preventive and health-promotion strategies targeting health-compromising behaviors such as drug abuse, high-risk sexual behavior, and accidental injury.

Wilson, D. K., Rodrigue, J. R., & Taylor, W. C. (Eds.) (1997). Health-promotion and health-compromising behaviors among minority adolescents. Washington, DC: American Psychological Association.

This volume describes culturally sensitive approaches for health psychologists who work with minority adolescents. Chapters summarize biological, social, cultural, and psychological perspectives on minority adolescent health as well as intervention programs targeting health-promotion and health-compromising behaviors.

True-False Questions

1. T   **F**   Approximately 30% of all highway fatalities are attributed to drinking and driving. (ref. p. 134)

2. **T**   F   It is estimated that one out of every ten adult Americans is an alcoholic or problem drinker. (ref. p. 135)

3. **T**   F   Psychological and social rewards associated with drinking include reduced anxiety and depression. (ref. p. 136)

4. T   **F**   Research supports the idea that most alcoholics eventually receive some form of inpatient or outpatient treatment. (ref. p. 141)

5. **T**   F   Trying cigarettes makes a person significantly more likely to use other drugs in the future. (ref. p. 145)

6. T   **F**   Because smoking increases social anxiety, relaxation training has been introduced to smoking cessation treatment. (ref. p. 155)

7. **T**   F   Smokers who believe that smoking helps them cope effectively with stress may be more vulnerable to relapse when under stress. (ref. p. 158)

8. **T**   F   Serotonin-enhancing substances, such as tryptophan and high-carbohydrate diets show therapeutic promise in smoking cessation programs. (ref. p. 158)

9. T   **F**   Research indicates that multimodal interventions are more effective in reducing smoking than social engineering strategies. (ref. p. 162)

10.   T   __F__   Passive smoking (i.e., secondhand smoke) is a documented health risk. (ref. p. 163)

Multiple-Choice Questions

1.   Alcohol abuse and smoking share a window of vulnerability in (ref. p. 132)
     a. adolescence
     b. young adulthood
     c. middle age
     d. old age

2.   Since he stopped smoking last week, John complains about fighting the urge for a cigarette, especially when he is around other smokers. This is an example of (ref. p. 133)
     a. addiction
     b. tolerance
     c. craving
     d. withdrawal

3.   Research on the nature of intravenous drug use indicates that sustained use is associated with (ref. p. 134)
     a. reduced euphoria
     b. increased tolerance
     c. distress related to discontinuing drug use
     d. all of the above

4.   Alcohol consumption has been linked to (ref. p. 134)
     a. cognitive impairment
     b. fetal alcohol syndrome
     c. some forms of cancer
     d. all of the above

5.   Alcoholics differ from problem drinkers in that alcoholics (ref. p. 135)
     a. show substantial social, psychological, and biomedical problems resulting from alcohol
     b. are defined by a variety of specific behaviors
     c. have a high tolerance for alcohol and show withdrawal symptoms when they attempt to become abstinent
     d. may have little ability to control their drinking

6.   Which of the following individuals would be **most** at risk for the development of alcoholism? (ref. p. 135)
     a. Shirley, whose identical twin, Fran, is an alcoholic
     b. George, whose fraternal twin, Sam, is an alcoholic
     c. Linda, whose adoptive mother, Gail, is an alcoholic
     d. Adam, whose father, Ben, is an alcoholic

7.   Alcohol abuse is known to depend on (ref. pp. 135–136)

    a. personal attitudes

    b. the social environment

    c. the cultural environment

    <u>d</u>. all of the above

8.   Individuals who experience _____ are more likely to become problem drinkers than those without these risk factors. (ref. p. 136)

    a. negative life events

    b. chronic stressors

    c. deficits in social support

    <u>d</u>. all of the above

9.   Alcohol consumption is associated with short-term reductions in (ref. p. 136)

    a. self-esteem

    b. positive affect

    <u>c</u>. negative affect

    d. all of the above

10.   Compared to persons with more long-term drinking problems, people who become problem drinkers in late middle age are (ref. p. 137)

    a. less likely to control their drinking on their own

    b. less likely to be successfully treated

    <u>c</u>. more likely to use problem drinking as a coping method

    d. all of the above

11.   Alcohol treatment programs (ref. p. 137)

    a. have low dropout rates

    b. are more successful with clients from low-SES backgrounds

    c. are more successful with female clients

    <u>d</u>. none of the above

12.   The goals of broad-spectrum cognitive-behavioral therapy of alcohol abuse include (ref. 137)

    a. reducing the reinforcement associated with alcohol

    b. teaching new behaviors inconsistent with alcohol abuse

    c. introducing reinforcement for activities that do not involve alcohol

    <u>d</u>. all of the above

13.   Placebo beverages that contain no alcohol are used in controlling craving. This is an example of (ref. p. 138)

    a. operant conditioning

    b. aversion therapy

    <u>c</u>. extinction training

    d. stimulus control

14. Relapsed alcoholics are more likely to have experienced negative life events than recovered alcoholics. This fact suggests that alcohol abuse treatment programs should include (ref. p. 140)

   <u>a</u>. skills training

   b. stimulus control

   c. contingency contracting

   d. aversion therapy

15. Residential alcohol treatment programs are (ref. pp. 137–141)

   a. superior to outpatient programs as they provide the controlled environment all alcoholics require

   <u>b</u>. necessary for alcoholics who require detoxification

   c. best suited for socially stable alcoholics

   d. all of the above

16. Alcoholics Anonymous (ref. p. 141)

   a. is a broad-spectrum treatment program

   <u>b</u>. is a self-help group

   c. has demonstrated lower dropout and relapse rates than inpatient programs

   d. all of the above

17. Studies of controlled drinking indicate that (ref. pp. 141–142)

   a. controlled or moderate drinking is impossible for all alcoholics

   b. abstinence is a more realistic social behavior for the social environments likely to be encountered by the recovered problem drinker

   c. programs that emphasize abstinence have lower dropout rates than programs that emphasize controlled drinking

   <u>d</u>. focused treatment programs of controlled drinking can be successful with some problem drinkers

18. Evaluations of alcohol prevention programs for adolescents suggest that such programs (ref. p. 142)

   a. are expensive and ineffective

   <u>b</u>. enhance participants' sense of self-efficacy

   c. are effective in changing participants' attitudes but have little influence on their ability to resist peer pressure

   d. none of the above

19. McGuire's (1982) review of drinking driver treatment programs concluded that most were successful in treating _____ . (ref. p. 143)

   <u>a</u>. light drinkers

   b. heavy drinkers

   c. low-SES drinkers

   d. high-SES drinkers

20. Moderate alcohol intake has been associated with (ref. p. 144)

   a. increased risk from coronary artery disease

   b. increased risk for cardiovascular disease

   <u>c</u>. elevated levels of high-density lipoprotein cholesterol (HDLC)

   d. elevated levels of low-density lipoprotein cholesterol (LDLC)

21.   _____ is/are the single greatest cause of preventable death. (ref. p. 145)
      a.   Obesity
      b.   Alcoholism
      c.   Vehicular accidents
      <u>d.</u>   Smoking

22.   Smoking and serum cholesterol interact to produce higher rates of morbidity and mortality by (ref. p. 146)
      <u>a.</u>   decreasing high-density lipoprotein production
      b.   increasing low-density lipoprotein production
      c.   inhibiting the blood's ability to coagulate
      d.   all of the above

23.   Following the publication of the Surgeon General's report on smoking in 1964, (ref. p. 146)
      a.   smoking in all groups has continued to increase
      b.   smoking in all groups has continued to increase, but the rate of increase has slowed
      <u>c.</u>   men's smoking has declined, but women's has increased
      d.   smoking among older people was relatively unaffected, but the percentage of teenage smokers has declined

24.   In the United States, smoking rates among (ref. p. 147)
      a.   men are especially low
      b.   men have increased since the 1940s
      c.   adolescents have been decreasing over the past five years
      <u>d.</u>   low-SES ethnic minority groups are especially high

25.   Smoking among adolescents is (ref. p. 148)
      a.   independent of other health-compromising behaviors
      <u>b.</u>   likely to occur in the presence of peers
      c.   an effort to maintain a positive mood
      d.   unrelated to individual differences in personality

26.   According to _____, smoking is reinforcing because nicotine stimulates reward centers in the nervous system. (ref. p. 151)
      a.   the nicotine regulation theory
      <u>b.</u>   the nicotine fixed-effect theory
      c.   the multiple regulation model
      d.   Pomerleau and Pomerleau's theory

27.   Critics of the nicotine regulation theory argue that (ref. p. 151)
      a.   smokers do not alter their smoking behavior enough to compensate for changes in pH level
      b.   smoking responds to environmental changes before environmental forces can affect urinary pH
      c.   smokers often relapse long after urinary nicotine levels are at zero
      <u>d.</u>   all of the above

28. According to the multiple regulation model (ref. p. 151)

   a. an understanding of the interactions of physiological, psychological factors is necessary to explain smoking

   b. emotional factors are central to smoking and nicotine becomes conditioned to emotional states

   c. smoking regulates a number of psychophysiological mechanisms in the body, all of which respond to nicotine

   d. smoking maintains a constant level of nicotine, which regulates performance and affect

29. After smoking for 20 years, Lucille has quit cold turkey. She complains, however, of having difficulty concentrating, impaired memory, and general anxiety and tension. In addition, she finds that smoking helped her cope with her stressful job in labor relations. Her response to quitting is best explained by (ref. pp. 151–152)

   a. the nicotine regulation theory

   b. the nicotine fixed-effect theory

   c. the multiple-regulation model

   d. Pomerleau and Pomerleau's theory

30. Evaluations of the effect of mass media antismoking messages suggest that they (ref. p. 152)

   a. provide information to smokers about health habits and are effective in persuading them to quit

   b. provide information about health habits to the general population but have little effect on anyone's behavior

   c. promote antismoking attitudes but have little effect upon smokers' behavioral intentions

   d. provide information about health habits and discourage nonsmokers from beginning to smoke

31. In contrast to nicotine gum, the use of transdermal nicotine patches (ref. p. 154)

   a. produces a sharper rise in nicotine level than does cigarette smoking

   b. does not produce significant gains in smoking cessation

   c. is associated with higher rates of patient compliance

   d. is more strongly associated with cardiovascular risk than smoking is

32. Focused smoking is a form of (ref. p. 154)

   a. aversion therapy

   b. operant conditioning

   c. contingency contracting

   d. nicotine replacement therapy

33. John is participating in a smoking cessation program. His counselor has placed John in a room with warm, smoky air where he inhales from a cigarette rapidly every few seconds while concentrating on the resulting negative effects. This is an example of (ref. p. 154)

   a. Emetine

   b. heavy smoking

   c. focused smoking

   d. rapid smoking

34. In which stage of Prochaska's transtheoretical model of behavior change would providing smokers with information about the adverse health consequences of smoking be the most effective? (ref. p. 155)

    a. precontemplation

    b. contemplation

    c. action

    d. preparation

35. The best predictor of long-term abstinence among smokers is (ref. p. 156)

    a. social support

    b. environmental support

    c. self-efficacy

    d. remaining vigilant about not smoking

36. Programs that provide materials to smokers so that they can quit on their own (ref. p. 158)

    a. are too haphazard in nature to be successful

    b. have been found to have higher initial quit rates than cognitive-behavioral interventions

    c. have been found to be as successful as cognitive-behavioral interventions in terms of long-term maintenance

    d. have the same impact as cognitive-behavioral interventions but are not as cost effective

37. Signs of withdrawal related to smoking cessation include (ref. p. 158)

    a. decreased heart rate and blood pressure, and increased epinephrine and norepinephrine levels

    b. increased heart rate and blood pressure, and increased epinephrine and norepinephrine levels

    c. decreased heart rate and blood pressure, and decreased epinephrine and norepinephrine levels

    d. increased heart rate and blood pressure, and decreased epinephrine and norepinephrine levels

38. Weight gains that follow smoking cessation may be related to changes in eating habits. Specifically, individuals who stop smoking (ref. p. 159)

    a. show a shift in preference for sweet, highly caloric foods

    b. show a shift in preference for high-fat, highly caloric foods

    c. show a shift in preference for a higher set point

    d. become more sensitive to external food-related cues

39. Weight gains following smoking cessation have been related to (ref. p. 159)

    a. changes in energy utilization following withdrawal from nicotine

    b. stress-induced eating

    c. changes in food habits

    d. all of the above

40. Most people quit smoking through (ref. p. 159)
   a. self-help groups
   b. work site interventions
   c. commercial stop-smoking clinics
   <u>d</u>. their own efforts

41. Those who quit smoking on their own (ref. p. 159)
   <u>a</u>. appear to be more successful in maintaining abstinence than participants in smoking cessation programs
   b. have high levels of self-control that is related to low relapse rates
   c. are more likely to have a socially supportive network that smokes
   <u>d</u>. have strong beliefs in the health benefits of stopping smoking

42. Social intervention programs frequently use the principle of behavioral inoculation. According to this principle, exposing individuals to a (ref. p. 160)
   a. strong persuasive message ensures that they will internalize the message
   b. boring, repetitive persuasive message ensures that they will become desensitized to the message
   c. one-sided message ensures that uncommitted individuals will more likely be persuaded by the message
   <u>d</u>. weak version of a persuasive message ensures that they will develop counterarguments to resist a stronger version of the message

43. The antismoking material included in Evans's (1988) adolescent smoking intervention program emphasized (ref. p. 161)
   a. the negative effects of smoking on long-term health
   b. the negative effects of smoking on longevity
   <u>c</u>. the negative effects of smoking on immediate health
   d. all of the above

44. Evaluation of social influence programs suggests that (ref. p. 161)
   a. adolescent smoking rates are unaffected
   b. fewer adolescents begin smoking after exposure to such programs
   <u>c</u>. adolescent smoking rates are reduced for up to four years
   d. none of the above

45. Passive smoking (second-hand smoke) has been found to be associated with (ref. p. 163)
   a. elevated blood carbon monoxide levels
   b. reduced pulmonary functioning
   c. increased rates of lung cancer
   <u>d</u>. all of the above

Essay Questions

1. Many health-compromising behaviors hare several important characteristics. Describe these characteristics and the implications for intervention programs. (ref. pp. 132–133)

2. Identify and describe the biological, psychological, and sociocultural factors implicated in alcohol abuse. (ref. pp. 135–137)

3. Explain the problem of relapse in the treatment of alcohol abuse. Which intervention strategies address this problem most effectively? Substantiate your answer with research from the text. (ref. pp. 138–141)

4. Answer the question posed in the text: Why is smoking so hard to change? (ref. pp. 158–159).

5. Describe the factors associated with smoking in adolescence. Evaluate the effectiveness of prevention programs targeting adolescents. (ref. pp. 149–150; 159–164;)

CHAPTER 6
WHAT IS STRESS?

Chapter Outline

I. Stress Defined

    A.   Early Contributions to the Study of Stress

    B.   Selye's General Adaptation Syndrome

    C.   Psychological Appraisal and the Experience of Stress

    D.   The Physiology of Stress

        1.   Assessing Stress

II. What Makes Events Stressful?

    A.   Dimensions of Stressful Events

    B.   Must Stress Be Perceived As Such to Be Stressful?

    C.   Can People Adapt to Stress?

    D.   Must a Stressor Be Ongoing to Be Stressful?

III. How Stress Has Been Studied

    A.   Stressful Life Events

    B.   Daily Stress

        1.   Chronic Strain

    C.   Stress in the Workplace

        1.   Stressful Job Factors

        2.   Occupational Stress, Illness, and Organizational Outcomes

        3.   Reducing Occupational Stress

    D.   Work Stress and Families

Learning Objectives

1. Define stress and stressors.
2. Trace the history of the study of stress.
3. Describe Cannon's fight-or-flight response.

4. Describe Selye's General Adaptation Syndrome.

5. Compare and contrast primary and secondary appraisal and their roles in the experience of stress.

6. Describe the physiological response to stress.

7. Describe the assessment of stress.

8. Describe the dimensions of stressful events.

9. Evaluate the extent to which stress is an objective versus subjective experience.

10. Explain the process of habituation to stress and responses to ongoing stressors.

11. Explain the relationship between arousal, emotional functioning, helplessness, and stress.

12. Describe the nature of stressful life events and their relationship to stress.

13. Describe the use of the Schedule of Recent Life Events (SRE) in the measurement of stress.

14. Define daily hassles and chronic strain and explain their relationship to physical and psychological health.

15. Describe factors in the workplace that are related to stress.

16. Describe the use of job enrichment to reduce occupational stress.

17. Explain the relationship of multiple roles to stress, and identify gender differences in work and family roles and the experience of stress.

Lecture Suggestions

Learned Helplessness and Health Psychology

Christopher Peterson presents a theoretical review of Seligman's original theory of learned helplessness and the more recent attributional model of learned helplessness, which has been written specifically for health psychologists. This review article can provide the basis for a lecture that reviews the two models and discusses the relationship of learned helplessness to health and illness. Applications of explanatory style to other health-related behaviors may be found in Buchanan and Seligman (1997).

Buchanan, G. McC., & Seligman, M. E. P. (1997). Explanatory style. Hillsdale, NJ: Erlbaum.
Peterson, C. (1982). Learned helplessness and health psychology. Health Psychology, 1, 153–168.

The Relationship of the Self-Concept to the Evaluation of Life Events

Some of the most stressful events may be those stressors that threaten one's identity and self-concept. According to Brown and McGill (1989), life events may have a negative effect on physical health only when they threaten one's self-image. They present an identity disruption model of stress, which posits that physical health and illness will be affected only by life events that are inconsistent with the self-concept. In this analysis, positive life events may have a detrimental effect on physical health only when they are experienced by persons with low self-esteem.

Brown, J. D., & McGill, K. L. (1989). The cost of good fortune: When positive life events produce negative health consequences. <u>Journal of Personality and Social Psychology</u>, <u>57</u>, 1103–1110.

Exercises, Projects, and Activities

The Experience of Stress

The topic of stress may be introduced through class discussion. Ask students about their personal experiences under stress. The following list of questions has been developed to encourage discussion of the roles that physiological arousal, appraisal, and life events play in the experience of stress.

1. How do you know when you're under stress?

2. What does stress feel like?

3. How does stress differ from anticipation? Excitement? Other emotions?

4. Can positive events be stressful? How?

Daily Hassles and Uplifts

The text's discussion of life events and hassles may be supplemented by administering the hassles and uplifts scales in class. The complete scales and scoring and normative information are available in Kanner, Coyne, Schaefer, and Lazarus (1981).

Kanner, A., Coyne, J. C., Schaefer, C., & Lazarus, R. S. (1981). Comparison of two modes of stress measurement: Daily hassles and uplifts versus major life events. <u>Journal of Behavioral Medicine</u>, <u>4</u>, 1–39.

Stress Log

The following assignment has been designed to provide a review of models of stress, the role of appraisal, and perceived control in the experience of stress. A complementary assignment that requires students to evaluate their log in terms of coping styles is described in Chapter 8.

For this assignment, review the text's description of various models of stress. Keep a log of events that most people would think might produce stress (everything that ranges from minor hassles to major annoyances) for at least 3 days. Be sure to hand in your log with this assignment. In addition to your log of stressful events, consider any other factors that might influence the effects of these events (e.g., positive events). Discuss the contents of your log in relation to the following points.

1. Apply Lazarus's model (<u>all aspects</u>) to explain whether these events were actually related to the subjective experience of stress in your case.

2. Were there any factors that buffered the effects of these stressors? What were they? Why do you feel they reduced your perceptions of stress?

3. Discuss the role perceived control may have played in your perception of stress.

Recommended Reading

Barnett, R. C., Biener, L., & Baruch, G. K. (1987). <u>Gender, stress, and health</u>. New York: Free Press/Macmillan.

This collection of writings summarizes the research investigating gender differences in stress, health, coping, and adaptation. Chapters are grouped into five sections: biosocial background, social roles and life events, specific stressors, coping, and adaptation.

Baum, A., & Singer, J. E. (Eds.). (1987). <u>Handbook of psychology and health: Vol. V. Stress</u>. Hillsdale: Erlbaum.

An advanced review of selected issues in stress research. Topics include the nature of stress, occupational stress, and stress management through exercise regimens.

Friedman, H. S. (Ed.). (1990). <u>Personality and disease</u>. New York: Wiley.

A collection of reviews and theoretical papers addressing general conceptual issues related to stress, emotion and health, and personality. Each chapter is authored by a prominent contributor to the field.

Lovallo, W. R. (1997). <u>Stress and health: Biological and psychological interactions</u>. Thousand Oaks, CA: Sage Publications.

Lovallo's book provides an overview of stress from the perspective of behavioral medicine. He begins with a review of the mind-body dichotomy and reviews the psychophysiological relationships between psychological processes and the stress response.

Selye, H. (1976). <u>The stress of life</u>. New York: McGraw-Hill.

This classic volume presents Selye's model of the general adaptation syndrome to a popular audience.

Smith, J. C. (1993). <u>Understanding stress and coping</u>. New York: Macmillan

This introductory text presents an overview of the research in stress and stressors and discusses the relationship between stress, health, and illness. Also included are specialized chapters addressing coping with disasters and crises, domestic and occupational stress, and active coping strategies.

True-False Questions

1. T   <u>F</u>   One of the earliest contributions to stress research was Hans Selye's fight-or-flight response. (ref. p. 169)

2. T   <u>F</u>   During the alarm phase of the general adaptation syndrome, the organism makes efforts to cope with the threat. (ref. p. 170)

3. <u>T</u>   F   Individual differences have been observed in reactivity and recovery following stress. (ref. p. 175)

4. T   <u>F</u>   Compared to positive events, negative events show a stronger relationship to psychological distress but not physical symptoms. (ref. p. 177)

5.   T   F   People who are heavily invested in several different roles may be better buffered from stress-related depression than those who are not. (ref. p. 178)

6.   T   F   Research suggests that habituation may not occur after exposure to long-term stressors and that the immune system may be particularly compromised by long-term stress. (ref. p. 179)

7.   T   F   The Schedule of Recent Life Events (SRE) currently is the most commonly used paper-and-pencil measure of stress. (ref. p. 189)

8.   T   F   According to a study by McGonagle and Kessler (1990), chronic strain may be more strongly related to depression than acute stress. (ref. p. 193)

9.   T   F   The perception of work overload shows a stronger relationship to physical health complaints and psychological distress than does objective measurements of workload. (ref. p. 195)

10. T   F   Research on multiple roles and stress among working parents indicate that men and women report being distressed by similar types of events. (ref. p. 199)

Multiple-Choice Questions

1.   Stress can be defined as a negative emotional experience accompanied by (ref. p. 168)
     a. biochemical and physiological changes
     b. cognitive changes
     c. behavioral changes
     d. all of the above

2.   Which of the following could be considered a stressor? (ref. p. 168)
     a. noise
     b. crowding
     c. commuting to work
     d. all of the above

3.   Most definitions of stress focus on (ref. p. 169)
     a. stressful events
     b. physiological changes
     c. emotional changes
     d. the relationship between the person and the environment

4.   The fight-or-flight response (ref. p. 169)
     a. is never adaptive
     b. involves arousal of the parasympathetic nervous system and the endocrine system
     c. involves arousal of the sympathetic nervous system and the endocrine system
     d. is subject to large individual differences

5.   Selye's (1956, 1976) studies of the general adaptation syndrome investigated _____ responses to stress. (ref. p. 169)
     a. psychological
     b. gastrointestinal
     c. adrenomedullary
     d. adrenocortical

6. The correct sequence of phases of the general adaptation syndrome is (ref. p. 170)

    <u>a</u>. alarm, resistance, exhaustion

    b. exhaustion, resistance, alarm

    c. resistance, alarm, exhaustion

    d. resistance, exhaustion, alarm

7. According to Selye (1956, 1976), the _____ phase of the general adaptation syndrome is responsible for the physiological damage related to stress. (ref. p. 170)

    a. alarm

    b. resistance

    <u>c</u>. exhaustion

    d. all of the above

8. According to its critics, Selye's (1956, 1976) model (ref. pp. 170)

    a. fails to offer a general theory of reactions to a wide variety of stressors over time

    b. fails to offer a physiological mechanism for the stress-illness relationship

    c. places too much emphasis on individual differences in response to stress

    <u>d</u>. fails to consider the role of psychological appraisal in stress

9. The process of primary appraisal involves the evaluation of one's (ref. p. 171)

    a. current emotional state

    <u>b</u>. perception of the event

    c. coping ability

    d. resources

10. The process of secondary appraisal involves the evaluation of one's (ref. p. 172)

    a. current emotional state

    b. perception of the event

    <u>c</u>. coping ability and resources

    d. all of the above

11. According to Lazarus's model, the subjective experience of stress is a result of (ref. p. 172)

    a. the general adaptation syndrome

    b. primary appraisal

    c. secondary appraisal

    <u>d</u>. the balance between primary and secondary appraisal

12. The adrenal cortex produces _____ in response to stress. (ref. p. 173)

    a. epinephrine and norepinephrine

    <u>b</u>. corticosteroids

    c. endogenous opioids

    d. ACTH

13. Activation of the hypothalamic-pituitary-adrenocortical (HPA) axis results in the secretion of (ref. p. 172–173)

    a. catecholamines

    b. norepinephrine

    <u>c</u>. corticosteroids

    d. all of the above

14. Research suggests that reactivity is related to individual differences in (ref. p. 175)
    a. acute and chronic illness
    b. psychological responses to stressors
    c. primary and secondary appraisal
    d. all of the above

15. _____ measures of stress have been found to predict psychological distress and illness. (ref. p. 177)
    a. Objective
    b. Subjective
    c. Both objective and subjective
    d. Ambiguous

16. Which of the following situations would be **least** stressful? (ref. pp. 177–178)
    a. Jill has filed for divorce after 25 years of marriage.
    b. Joe arrives at his first class of the day to find that the professor will administer a pop quiz.
    c. Linda, a full-time college student, finds that she will have to find a second part-time job due to cuts in financial aid packages.
    d. Karl, a file clerk, has been working intensively for 3 weeks on a new job responsibility.

17. Feelings of control (ref. p. 177)
    a. decrease the subjective experience of stress but have no effect on the physiological response
    b. may decrease initial perceptions of stress, but need to be supplemented with additional resources for long-term coping
    c. may increase initial perceptions of stress but also augment coping
    d. are unrelated to measures of self-efficacy

18. Occupational stress may be related to (ref. p. 178)
    a. role ambiguity
    b. role overload
    c. contradictory standards
    d. all of the above

19. Studies of children exposed to noisy environments indicate that children (ref. p. 181)
    a. eventually habituate to high levels of noise
    b. exposed to noise exhibit performance decrements and learned helplessness
    c. exposed to noise exhibit few cognitive decrements but do show signs of learned helplessness
    d. eventually learn to change their task strategies and attentional focus to accommodate the noise in their environments

20. The aftereffects of stress are most pronounced when the stressor is (ref. p. 182)
    a. negative
    b. intense
    c. anticipated
    d. unpredictable

21. Mort complains that his job-related stress makes it difficult to focus on other problems, shortens his attention span, and makes him feel as if he has little time and energy for other areas of his life. Mort's description most closely resembles the _____ theory of stress. (ref. p. 182)

a. cognitive costs
b. physiological arousal
c. emotional response
d. learned helplessness

22. Post-traumatic stress disorder (PTSD) has been associated with (ref. p. 184)

a. temporary changes in the brain involving the amygdala
b. decreased cortisol, norepinephrine and epinephrine
c. biochemical and hormonal alterations that last over a long period of time
d. all of the above

23. Learned helplessness is associated with _____ deficits. (ref. pp. 182–185)

a. motivational
b. cognitive
c. emotional
d. all of the above

24. In their study of dormitory crowding, Baum and Valins concluded that students developed learned helplessness as a result of (ref. p. 185)

a. sustained levels of arousal
b. high levels of intermittent noise
c. uncontrollable personal interactions
d. all of the above

25. According to Holmes and Rahe (1967), an event is potentially stressful if it (ref. p. 186)

a. is negative
b. threatens one's self-concept
c. is long-term
d. requires adaptation

26. Which of the following would be considered a stressful life event? (ref. p. 186)

a. lack of career fulfillment
b. a significant change in job responsibilities
c. questioning one's identity and goals
d. all of the above

27. The relationship between scores on the Schedule of Recent Life Events (SRE) and illness is (ref. p. 186)

a. negligible
b. modest
c. robust
d. unpredictable

28. Which of the following is a valid criticism of Holmes and Rahe's (1967) Schedule of Recent Life Events (SRE)? (ref. p. 186–188)

   a. It is uncorrelated with illness and health behaviors.

   b. It fails to consider individual differences in the experience and reporting of events.

   c. It contains life events that are confounded with health and ongoing strain, thus underestimating the actual correlation between health and illness.

   d. It fails to consider that the number of illnesses experienced over a period of time is more important than the severity and the duration of these illnesses.

29. Which of the following is **not** a valid criticism of Holmes and Rahe's (1967) Schedule of Recent Life Events (SRE)? (ref. pp. 186–188)

   a. Some of the items on the list are too specific.

   b. Individual differences in the experience of events are not taken into account.

   c. It treats both positive and negative events in a similar fashion.

   d. It does not assess whether events have been resolved or not.

30. The occurrence of daily hassles (ref. p. 189)

   a. bears no relationship to physical health

   b. reduces psychological well-being over the short term

   c. markedly enhances reports of physical symptoms

   d. are poorer predictors of physical health than major life events

31. Hassles are minor life events that (ref. p. 189)

   a. have a cumulative effect on health and illness

   b. are not confounded with mental and physical illness

   c. have an objective, but not subjective, component

   d. all of the above

32. The cumulative impact of daily hassles may be particularly pronounced for individuals who are prone to react to stress with (ref. p. 190)

   a. optimism

   b. Type A behavior

   c. anxiety

   d. depression

33. Sudden death (e.g., nightmare death) appears to be explained by (ref. p. 191)

   a. a sex-linked genetic disorder

   b. night terrors

   c. a preexisting somatic weakness paired with unexpected, uncontrollable shock

   d. pressures of adjusting to American life

34. Terry is involved in a long-term but ultimately unsatisfying relationship with Lee. This is an example of (ref. p. 190)

   a. a stressor

   b. a life event

   c. daily hassles

   d. chronic strain

35. Chronic strain appears to (ref. p. 193)
    <u>a</u>. mediate the impact of negative life events
    b. habituate people to negative life events
    c. be unrelated to negative life events
    d. be unrelated to illness

36. <u>Karoshi</u> refers to (ref. p. 194)
    a. sudden nocturnal death
    <u>b</u>. death from overwork
    c. stress-related mental illness
    d. none of the above

37. Workers who suffer from work overload _____ compared with workers who do not experience overload. (ref. p. 194)
    a. feel more stressed
    b. practice poorer health habits
    c. sustain more health risks
    <u>d</u>. all of the above

38. Air traffic controllers experience a great deal of occupational stress due to the _____ associated with this occupation. (ref. p. 195)
    a. role ambiguity
    <u>b</u>. responsibility for others
    c. number of job demands
    d. role conflict

39. Mike has been having difficulty meeting the demands of two executives who oversee his work area and communicate conflicting expectations. One executive is concerned about production and constantly urges Mike to meet performance quotas. The other is concerned about quality assurance and would like Mike to slow down and focus on the quality of his work. This is an example of (ref. p. 195)
    a. role ambiguity
    <u>b</u>. role conflict
    c. work pressure
    d. all of the above

40. The effects of unemployment (ref. p. 197)
    a. are unaffected by social support
    <u>b</u>. include increased vulnerability to other life events
    c. include psychological but not physical symptoms
    d. all of the above

41. Research suggests that substance abuse and decreased quantity and quality of work are related to (ref. p. 250)
    a. specific job characteristics
    b. active involvement in decision making
    <u>c</u>. ways of coping with stress and alienation
    d. all of the above

42. Job enrichment programs are designed to (ref. p. 198)
    a. reduce job unpredictability and ambiguity
    b. increase job interest and involvement
    c. increase positive social interaction with coworkers
    d. reward workers for productivity rather than punish them for defects

43. Researchers investigating the effects of multiple roles on women conclude that (ref. p. 199)
    a. outside employment can be beneficial for women's well-being
    b. having control and flexibility over the work environment reduces the likelihood of stress
    c. work that is satisfying and enjoyable is protective against psychological distress
    d. all of the above

44. Higher levels of stress are reported by working parents who experience (ref. p. 199)
    a. inequitable sharing of household and childcare responsibilities.
    b. high levels of job complexity
    c. good income
    d. flexible work schedules

45. For men _____ moderates the stress-illness relationship. (ref. p. 199)
    a. employment
    b. marriage
    c. satisfaction with the parent role
    d. all of the above

Essay Questions

1. Describe Lazarus's model of the role of psychological appraisal in the experience of stress. Explain how this model addresses the cognitive and emotional responses to stress. (ref. pp. 171–172)

2. Explain how the sympathetic-adrenomedullary (SAM) and hypothalamic-pituitary-adrenocortical (HPA) axis are implicated in the physiological response to stress. (ref. pp. 172–175).

3. Answer the text's question "what makes events stressful?" (ref. pp. 177–179)

4. A group of friends is discussing the different ways in which life can "get at you." Pat says it's the milestones in life that are most stressful, illustrating this point by describing several traumatic divorces and untimely deaths from which family members have yet to recover. On the other hand, Lee asserts that it's the little, constant annoyances in life that are most harmful to psychological and physical health, citing the annoyance experienced while commuting to work everyday or coping with an intrusive landlord. Evaluate both of these arguments, citing research from the text. (ref. pp. 185–194)

5. Some working parents cope well with their multiple roles whereas others do not. Explain the factors that are associated with positive and negative outcomes in juggling family and work roles. (ref. pp. 199–200)

CHAPTER 7

MODERATORS OF THE STRESS EXPERIENCE

Chapter Outline

I. Stress and Illness

II. Coping with Stress

    A. Personality and Coping

        1. Negativity, Stress, and Illness

        2. Hardiness

        3. Optimism

        4. Psychological Control

    B. Additional Coping Resources

    C. Coping Style

        1. Avoidance Versus Confrontation

        2. Disclosure

    D. Coping Strategies

III. Coping and External Resources

    A. Social Support

        1. What Is Social Support?

        2. Effect of Social Support on Psychological Distress

        3. Effect of Social Support on Illness and Health Habits

        4. Moderation of Stress by Social Support

        5. Providing Effective Social Support

        6. Treats to Social Support

        7. Biopsychosocial Pathways

IV. Coping Outcomes

V. The Management of Stress

A.   Basic Techniques of Stress Management

B.   Relaxation Training and Stress Management

C.   Supplementary Stress Management Skills

Learning Objectives

1.   Define stress moderators.

2.   Describe how stress may exert a direct effect on illness, interact with pre-existing vulnerabilities, and adversely affect health habits.

3.   Define the coping process.

4.   Define negativity and the pessimistic explanatory style and explain their relationship to stress and illness.

5.   Define hardiness and optimism and explain their relationship to stress and illness.

6.   Describe the relationship of psychological control to stress and illness.

7.   Describe the relationship of other personality variables (e.g., self-esteem and conscientiousness) to stress and illness.

8.   Define avoidance and confrontative coping styles and explain their relationship to stress and illness.

9.   Explain the relationship of disclosure to coping with stress and illness.

10. Compare and contrast different coping strategies and explain their relationship to stress and illness.

11. Describe the role of external resources in coping and their relationship to stress and illness.

12. Define social support. Compare and contrast the different forms of social support.

13. Describe the effect of social support on psychological distress, illness and health habits.

14. Explain how stress is moderated by social support. Compare and contrast the direct effects and buffering hypotheses.

15. Describe the factors affecting the provision of effective social support.

16. Explain the biopsychosocial pathways by which social support influences health and illness.

17. Describe the tasks and costs of coping. Explain the criteria by which coping outcomes are assessed.

18. Define stress management and describe the nature of stress management programs.

19. Describe the basic techniques of stress management.

20. Describe relaxation training and evaluate its effectiveness.

21. Describe the use of time management and assertiveness training in stress management programs.

Lecture Suggestions

Excuses and Illusions of Personal Control

Snyder and his colleagues' (Snyder & Higgins, 1988; Snyder, Higgins, & Stucky, 1983) studies of the adaptive nature of excuses and other self-enhancing attributions suggest that attributions play an important role in the appraisal of negative events. They argue that excuses serve an important psychological function by protecting one's self-esteem and maintaining a sense of personal control. Further, they assert that providing excuses for one's negative behavior may reduce stress and have a positive effect on both psychological functioning and physical health. This topic may stir debate about the conditions under which denial and self-protective cognitions may be adaptive and the circumstances under which they may undermine healthy psychological functioning (e.g., Baumeister, 1989; Lazarus, 1983).

Baumeister, R. F. (1989). The optimal margin of illusion. Journal of Social and Clinical Psychology, 8, 176–189.

Lazarus, R. S. (1983). The costs and benefits of denial. In S. Bresnitz (Ed.), Denial of stress (pp. 1–32). New York: International Universities Press.

Snyder, C. R., & Higgins, R. L. (1988). Excuses: Their effective role in the negotiation of reality. Psychological Bulletin, 104, 23–35.

Snyder, C. R., Higgins, R. L., & Stucky, R. J. (1983). Excuses: Masquerades in search of grace. New York: Wiley.

Conceptualizing Social Support

As the text notes, social support is a complex psychosocial variable. Wortman and Dunkel-Schetter (1987) present a review of this construct that is useful in developing a lecture to present to students the conceptual and methodological issues surrounding this construct. Another excellent instructor resource is Cohen's (1988) review of the literature. In addition, it may be useful to address the negative aspects of social support. Students often fail to consider the obligations that membership in a complex social network often places on the individual. DiMatteo and Hays (1981) discuss the harmful effects social support may have on family functioning, compliance, and patient self-esteem.

Cohen, S. (1988). Psychosocial models of the role of social support in the etiology of disease. Health Psychology, 7, 269–297.

DiMatteo, M. R., & Hays, R. (1981). Social support and illness. In B. H. Gottlieb (Ed.), Social networks and social support (pp. 117–148). Beverly Hills: Sage.

Wortman, C. B., & Dunkel-Schetter, C. (1987). Conceptual and methodological issues in the study of social support. In A. Baum & J. E. Singer (Eds.), Handbook of psychology and health: Vol. V. Stress (pp. 63–108). Hillsdale: Erlbaum.

Collective Coping

James Pennebaker and Kent Harber (1993) present a model of collective coping that may be useful in fostering class discussion of the coping process. On the basis of survey data collected from San Francisco residents who had experienced the Loma Prieta earthquake and

Dallas residents during and after the Persian Gulf conflict, Pennebaker and Harber developed a stage model of collective coping with social upheaval. They found that people talk and think about an event for approximately 2 weeks after it occurs (the emergency stage). Then, people move into an inhibition stage during which discussion is reduced but thinking and rumination continues. It is during this stage that negative reactions, such as hostility and dreaming, occur. Afterward, people progress into the adaptation phase where both discussion and thought about the event diminish.

Pennebaker, J. W., & Harber, K. D. (1993). A social stage model of collective coping: The Loma Prieta earthquake and the Persian Gulf War. Journal of Social Issues, 49, 125–145.

Coping with a Health Threat: Genetic Counseling

The relationship of personal control to coping may be reviewed by discussing research investigating how people cope with information about a potential health threat. A recent study (Shiloh, et al., 1997) illustrates the role of personal control and coping. It also provides an opportunity to discuss the differential effects of emotion-focused and problem-focused coping. It also may be used to integrate material from Chapter 2.

Shiloh, S., Berkenstadt, M., Meiran, N., Bat-Miriam-Katznelson, M., & Goldman, B. (1997). Mediating effects of perceived personal control in coping with a health threat: The case of genetic counseling. Journal of Applied Social Psychology, 27, 1146–1174.

Exercises, Projects, and Activities

Coping Styles and Strategies

The topic of coping may be introduced by asking students to list on the board the ways in which they typically handle stress. The similarities and differences of the individual coping strategies may then be discussed. Finally, categorize each strategy according to the Ways of Coping Scale criteria.

Assessing Coping Strategies

Student analyses of their daily coping strategies may form the basis of an independent assignment. This assignment may be integrated with the stress log discussed in Chapter 6. A sample assignment with suggested guidelines follows.

For this assignment, review your log of stressors that you handed in with Assignment _____ . Be sure to hand in your log again with this assignment. If you wish, you might monitor your stress and coping for another day or two to provide you with more information for your analysis. In addition to your log of stressful events, consider any other factors that you discussed in your earlier assignment (e.g., positive events). Write an essay that addresses the following points:

1. How did you cope with these events? Could you summarize your coping strategies according to a particular coping style(s)?

2. How successful were your coping efforts? Did some coping strategies work better than others? Were certain efforts more successful with certain stressors?

3. What role, if any, did social support play in your coping with stress? Were certain support efforts more effective than others? Why or why not?

4. Do you feel that stress management techniques might improve your coping? Which one(s)? Why?

Recommended Reading

Cohen, S., & Syme, S. L. (Eds.). (1985). Social support and health. New York: Academic Press.

This advanced text includes chapters on the study of social support, life-span perspectives on social support, social support and the etiology of disease, and social support interventions and health policy.

Friedman, H. S. (Ed.). (1992). Hostility, coping, and health. Washington, DC: American Psychological Association.

This edited volume presents recent research on the role of hostility in stress, coping, and health. Chapters address the nature and measurement of hostility, hostility and the coronary-prone personality, and the relationship of hostility to coping strategies.

Lazarus, R. S., & Folkman, S. (1984). Stress, appraisal, and coping. New York: Springer.

An excellent review of social and psychological processes related to stress. The authors discuss the role of cognitive appraisal and coping in stress and adaptation, stress management, and the relationship between cognition and emotions.

Taylor, S. E. (1990). Positive illusions: Creative self-deception and the healthy mind. New York: Basic Books.

A presentation of the roles perceived control, mastery, and self-enhancing attributions play in the maintenance of physical and mental health.

True-False Questions

1. T   <u>F</u>   According to Lazarus's view of stress, any new event or change in the environment prompts the individual to make secondary appraisals of the significance of the event. (ref. p. 204)

2. T   <u>F</u>   Negative affectivity has been related to alcoholism, depression, and suicidal behavior, but not poor health. (ref. pp. 205–206)

3. <u>T</u>   F   A sense of personal control may be the most important component of hardiness in terms of predicting good health. (ref. p. 208)

4. <u>T</u>   F   Optimism and hardiness are associated with the use of active coping strategies such as problem-focused coping. (ref. p. 208–209)

5. T   <u>F</u>   Coping styles are like personality traits in that they are thought to come into play primarily when events become stressful. (ref. p. 211)

6. T   <u>F</u>   Research has found that talking about one's troubles results in a short-term improvement of mood but has little long-term effect on health and illness. (ref. p. 215)

7. <u>T</u>   F   There appear to be developmental differences in general coping strategies as problem-focused coping appears to emerge during childhood, and emotion-focused coping develops somewhat later. (ref. p. 216)

8. T   <u>F</u>   Whereas social support is associated physical and psychological well-being, research has failed to establish a relationship between social support and good health habits . (ref. p. 224)

9. T   <u>F</u>   Overall, research investigating the effectiveness of social support fails to support the matching hypothesis. (ref. p. 226)

10. <u>T</u>   F   Ancillary skills of stress management include time management, good health habits, and social skills. (ref. p. 234–235)

Multiple-Choice Questions

1. Moderators of the stress experience may have an impact on (ref. p. 202)
    a. stress itself
    b. the relation between stress and illness
    c. the relation between stress and psychological responses
    <u>d</u>. all of the above

2. According to Tapp and Natelson's (1988) study of the impact of stress on hamsters with inherited heart disease, stress precipitated heart failure (ref. p. 203)
    a. when stress occurred early in the disease process
    <u>b</u>. when stress occurred after cardiac changes had time to develop
    c. because stress ws an additional burden for an animal with a physical vulnerability
    d. all of the above

3. According to the interactive model of the stress-illness relationship, (ref. p. 203)
    a. either stress or a pre-existing vulnerability is sufficient to produce illness
    b. experiencing stress causes individuals to become particularly vulnerable to illness
    <u>c</u>. stress leads to illness among individuals with a pre-existing vulnerability to illness
    d. the physiological changes associated with stress increase individual vulnerability to illness

4. Cohen and Williamson (1988) found that people under stress got less sleep, were less likely to eat breakfast, and consumed more drugs and alcohol than people not under stress. This study provides evidence that stress is related to illness due to changes in (ref. p. 203)
    a. secondary gain
    b. social interaction
    <u>c</u>. health behaviors
    d. illness behaviors

5.   The process of _____ involves the evaluation of one's resources to determine whether they will be sufficient to meet the demands of stressful situations or events. (ref. p. 204)

    a.   primary appraisal

    <u>b</u>.   secondary appraisal

    c.   coping

    d.   all of the above

6.   The process of _____ involves an individual's efforts to manage internal or external demands that tax his or her resources. (ref. p. 204)

    a.   primary appraisal

    b.   secondary appraisal

    <u>c</u>.   coping

    d.   all of the above

7.   The consideration of coping as a dynamic process implies that (ref. p. 204)

    a.   coping involves a wide range of actions and reactions to stress

    b.   coping efforts are moderated by personal resources

    c.   coping involves an ongoing set of responses by which the person continues to act on the environment

    <u>d</u>.   coping involves an ongoing set of responses by which the person and the environment are involved in a reciprocal interaction

8.   Individuals high in negative affectivity (ref. p. 205)

    <u>a</u>.   may be described as having a "disease-prone" personality

    b.   are more likely to seek out medical care for minor complaints

    c.   repress their stress-related symptoms but complain more about their general health

    d.   are characterized as being depressed, anxious, and psychotic

9.   According to Friedman and Booth-Kewley (1987), the "disease-prone" personality (ref. p. 205)

    a.   is characterized by a pessimistic explanatory style

    b.   is highly correlated with the presence of chronic diseases

    <u>c</u>.   may predispose people to certain chronic diseases

    d.   may be the result of long-term suffering from chronic diseases

10.   Individuals who are high in negative affectivity (ref. p. 206)

    a.   are less likely to use health services

    <u>b</u>.   are particularly likely to report physical symptoms

    c.   suppress symptoms of psychological distress and physical illness

    d.   all of the above

11.   An individual with a pessimistic explanatory style is more likely to interpret negative events in terms of _____ factors. (ref. p. 207)

    a.   external, unstable, specific

    b.   external, stable, global

    c.   internal, unstable, global

    <u>d</u>.   internal, stable, global

12. Wilma has experienced increasing levels of stress due to her deteriorating test scores in psychology. She complains to her friend Betty, "I can't seem to get the hang of this stuff. I'm just not smart enough. I may have to drop out of the university." Betty replies, "You're smart enough, Wilma, but you're just not spending enough time studying." Betty is trying to change Wilma's attributions of (ref. p. 207)

    a. internality
    b. stability
    c. globality
    d. all of the above

13. A study of elderly men and women conducted by Kamen-Siegel and colleagues (1991) found that pessimistic explanatory style is associated with (ref. p. 207)

    a. reduced immunocompetence
    b. higher rates of physical illness
    c. increased use of health facilities
    d. all of the above

14. Which of the following is **not** a component of hardiness? (ref. p. 208)

    a. commitment
    b. control
    c. challenge
    d. consistency

15. Hardy individuals (ref. p. 208)

    a. experience fewer stressful life events than other people
    b. may appraise potentially stressful events in a more positive fashion than other people
    c. protect themselves from stress by avoiding change and new activities
    d. none of the above

16. Hardy individuals are (ref. p. 208)

    a. more likely to use avoidant coping strategies
    b. more likely to use active coping strategies
    c. less likely to enlist social support
    d. none of the above

17. Of the following variables, _____ appear to be most strongly related to physical health. (ref. p. 208)

    a. commitment and challenge
    b. commitment and control
    c. challenge and control
    d. challenge and cognitive reappraisal

18. Critics of the hardiness concept have argued that this construct is confounded with (ref. p. 208)

    a. sensation-seeking
    b. time-urgency
    c. negative affectivity
    d. extroversion

19. Scheier, Weintraub, and Carver (1986) found that optimists may cope more effectively because they are more likely to use _____ as a coping strategy. (ref. p. 209)
    a. denial
    b. distancing
    c. problem-focused coping
    d. accepting personal responsibility

20. The belief that one can determine one's own internal states and behavior, influence one's environment, and/or bring about desired outcomes is (ref. p. 210)
    a. optimism
    b. personal control
    c. self-efficacy
    d. hardiness

21. Control has been related to (ref. p. 210)
    a. emotional well-being
    b. successful coping
    c. improved cognitive performance
    d. all of the above

22. High self-esteem has been related to (ref. p. 210)
    a. increased longevity
    b. active coping strategies
    c. reducing the harmful effects of high levels of stress
    d. reducing the harmful effects of low levels of stress

23. Research investigating the effectiveness of avoidant and vigilant coping strategies suggests that (ref. pp. 212–213)
    a. avoidant strategies are effective in dealing with long-term stressors
    b. vigilant copers may exhibit short-term anxiety but cope well with long-term stressors
    c. the use of vigilant or confrontative coping styles may represent a risk factor for negative responses to stressors
    d. both avoidant and vigilant strategies are equally effective in coping with stress

24. Researchers investigating catharsis have found that subjects who freely express their feelings about traumatic events (ref. p. 215)
    a. show increased levels of physiological arousal
    b. have difficulty maintaining adequate levels of social support
    c. are no longer upset about the events after expressing themselves
    d. are less likely to have subsequent health problems

25. According to your text, successful coping might best be determined by (ref. p. 216)
    a. an effective fit between coping strategy and stressor
    b. a reliance on problem-solving strategies rather than on emotional regulation
    c. individual differences in coping style
    d. minimizing the costs of coping

26. Emotion-focused efforts would be most effective in coping with the worry and stress due to (ref. p. 216)

   a. having two final exams scheduled for the same day

   <u>b</u>. waiting to hear if your application to graduate school has been accepted

   c. receiving a notice that your taxes will be audited by the IRS next week

   d. any of the above

27. In a recent twin study, Kendler and colleagues (1991) discovered that two coping strategies, turning to others and problem-solving, could be explained by (ref. pp. 216–217)

   a. early socialization

   b. parenting behaviors

   <u>c</u>. genetic factors

   d. all of the above

28. As assessed by the Ways of Coping instrument, which of the following coping strategies does **not** focus on emotional regulation? (ref. p. 217)

   a. self-control

   b. positive reappraisal

   <u>c</u>. seeking social support

   d. accepting responsibility

29. Ed's job has become increasingly stressful since a new supervisor has criticized even minor errors in his work. Finally, Ed sits down with his supervisor and says, "I am the most productive member of this team. You cannot continue to be overly critical of my work. It's unfair." This is an example of (ref. p. 217)

   <u>a</u>. confrontative coping

   b. planful problem-solving

   c. accepting responsibility

   d. self-control

30. Joan finds that she drinks more heavily now that she is going through the final stages of her divorce. The use of substances such as alcohol or cigarettes in an effort to relieve stress is an example of (ref. p. 217)

   a. self-control

   b. distancing

   c. seeking social support

   <u>d</u>. escape/avoidance

31. People who are higher in socioeconomic status (SES) show (ref. p. 221)

   a. lower morbidity for medical and psychiatric disorderes

   b. lower mortality from all causes of death

   c. superior immune functioning

   <u>d</u>. all of the above

32. Information from others that one is loved and cared for, esteemed and valued, and part of a network of communication and mutual obligation is (ref. p. 222)

    a. coping
    b. internal resources
    c. social support
    d. external resources

33. A patient with AIDS decides to enter therapy. He explains that the therapist helps him in ways his friends and family cannot. Specifically, his therapist helps him find ways to cope with the disorder and understand it. This is an example of (ref. p. 222)

    a. personal control
    b. appraisal support
    c. tangible assistance
    d. emotional support

34. Research evidence suggests that social support may reduce (ref. p. 223)

    a. the likelihood of becoming ill, but it has no effect on recovery rates or mortality
    b. the likelihood of becoming ill only indirectly by affecting health habits
    c. the likelihood of becoming ill, shorten recovery rates, and reduce mortality
    d. perceived psychological distress, but it has no effect on physical health or illness

35. According to the buffering hypothesis, (ref. p. 225)

    a. the more resources an individual has the better he or she is able to cope with stress
    b. individual resources augment one's ability to cope with high or low levels of stress
    c. individual resources improve a person's ability to cope with only moderate levels of stress
    d. individual resources have little effect on coping with low levels of stress but become important at high levels of stress

36. Evaluations of the effectiveness of social support have shown having a large number of close friends and family members (ref. p. 225)

    a. has a cumulative effect on physical health
    b. may contribute to stress in some cases
    c. is superior to having one close friend, especially for men
    d. none of the above

37. An important variable in understanding the mechanism by which stress is moderated by social support appears to be the manner in which social support is assessed. When social support has been measured in terms of social integration, _____ have been found. When subjective levels of social support have been assessed, however, _____ have been found. (ref. p. 225)

    a. direct effects; few effects
    b. buffering effects; few effects
    c. buffering effects; direct effects
    d. direct effects; buffering effects

38. According to Thoits (1986), one important characteristic of effective providers of social support is (ref. p. 226)
    a. emotional expressivity
    b. warmth and nurturance
    c. personal and social resources
    d. empathy

39. The idea that the effectiveness of social support is determined by the ability of an individual's social network to provide the particular types of assistance needed in times of stress is the (ref. p. 226)
    a. direct effects hypothesis
    b. buffering hypothesis
    c. matching hypothesis
    d. none of the above

40. Recently, a number of researchers have investigated the costs of providing social support. According to these studies, close friends or family members may encounter difficulties in providing social support if (ref. pp. 226–227)
    a. they attempt to provide a form of support that is inconsistent with their role
    b. the recipient of support is unaware or unappreciative of their efforts
    c. the social support needs of the providers are unmet
    d. all of the above

41. Researchers have found SAM and HPA activation and impaired immune system functioning among (ref. pp. 227)
    a. heterosexual couples during marital conflict
    b. family members with Alzheimer's disease
    c. careproviders for cancer patients
    d. widows who resent intrusive friends

42. Social support has beneficial effects on (ref. p. 228)
    a. cardiovascular system
    b. endocrine system
    c. immune system
    d. all of the above

43. The author of your text concludes that successful coping might be best conceptualized as the (ref. p. 229)
    a. sequential resolution of each of the relevant tasks of coping
    b. ongoing process of attempting to negotiate issues around which coping efforts are structured
    c. successful resolution of coping tasks
    d. mastery of specific tasks as measured by one specific criterion

44. Stress management programs (ref. p. 230)
    a. are best conducted on an individual basis by a licensed psychotherapist
    b. are effective in relieving psychological distress but are seldom used in the treatment of stress-related illnesses
    c. may be beneficial in controlling stress-related disorders and reducing risk factors associated with coronary heart disease
    d. may be beneficial in controlling stress-related disorders and psychological distress but have not yet been proven to be cost effective

45. Relaxation training is designed to (ref. p. 234)
    a. provide cognitive insights into the nature and control of stress
    b. reduce the physiological arousal associated with stress
    c. mitigate the effect of stress carriers
    d. all of the above

Essay Questions

1. Explain what is meant by the term "stress moderator." Identify three psychological variables and three social variables that have been found to moderate stress. Citing research from the text, explain the relationship between these variables and the experience of stress. (ref. pp. 202–229)

2. Explain how individual differences in personality are related to coping. (ref. pp. 205–211)

3. Explain how coping styles and coping strategies moderate the experience of stress. Citing research from the text, evaluate the effectiveness of each in terms of the type of stressor that a person might be faced with. (ref. pp. 211–217)

4. What is social support? What are the benefits of having a sufficient amount of social support? What are the costs of being in a dense social network? (ref. pp. 222–230)

5. Your dormitory suitemate is suffering from stress due to final exams. Using the techniques described in the text, design a simple stress management program. Explain the function of each component and why it should be included in the program. (ref. pp. 231–235)

CHAPTER 8
USING HEALTH SERVICES

Chapter Outline

I.   Recognition and Interpretation of Symptoms

      A.   Recognition of a Symptom

      B.   Interpretation of Symptoms

            1.   Prior Experience

            2.   Expectations

            3.   "Seriousness" of the Symptoms

      C.   Cognitive Representations of Illness

      D.   The Beginning of Treatment

II.   Who Uses Health Services?

III.   Misusing Health Services

      A.   Using Health Services for Emotional Disturbances

      B.   Delay Behavior

IV.   The Patient in the Hospital Setting

      A.   Structure of the Hospital

      B.   Functioning of the Hospital

      C.   Recent Changes in Hospitalization

      D.   The Impact of Hospitalization on the Patient

V.   Interventions to Increase Control in Hospital Settings

      A.   Coping with Surgery Through Control-Enhancing Interventions

      B.   Coping with Stressful Medical Procedures Through Control-Enhancing Interventions

VI.   The Hospitalized Child

      A.   Preparing Children for Medical Interventions

Learning Objectives

1. Describe the social and psychological factors that influence the recognition and interpretation of symptoms.

2. Define illness representations and illness schema, and explain their influence on the interpretation of symptoms.

3. Describe the nature and function of disease prototypes.

4. Describe the nature and function of the lay referral network.

5. Describe the demographic factors that predict the use of health services.

6. Describe the sociocultural factors that predict the use of health services.

7. Explain why people misuse health services for emotional disturbances.

8. Explain the nature and consequences of delay behavior.

9. Describe the nature of the hospital structure and functioning.

10. Explain recent changes in hospitalization that influence treatment.

11. Describe the impact of hospitalization on the patient.

12. Describe the hospital patient role and explain the relationship of personal control to reactance.

13. Describe the nature and effectiveness of control-enhancing interventions in helping patients cope with surgery and stressful medical procedures.

14. Describe reactions to hospitalization commonly observed in young children.

15. Describe the nature and effectiveness of control-enhancing interventions designed to help children cope with hospitalization and stressful medical procedures.

Lecture Suggestions

Medical Ageism

As the text notes, practitioners hold cognitive representations of illness and the patient prototypes. Thus, practitioner stereotypes about their patients may influence the diagnosis of symptoms as well as the quality of care provided to the patient. Gerontologists increasingly are concerned that practitioners who hold negative attitudes toward their elderly patients may attribute medical symptoms requiring treatment to reflect normal signs of aging (Kosberg, 1983). Conversely, ageist practitioners who hold negative expectations about the ability of older people to remain active and meet social role demands may overmedicate elderly patients (Williams, 1981). Two recent studies indicate that geriatric training had little effect upon attitudes (Brooks, 1993; Saarela & Viukari, 1995) A classroom discussion of these issues would be most effective if it integrated practitioner attitudes toward their patients within the context of practitioner socialization in professional training (see Coccaro & Miles, 1984) and the changing nature of the health care delivery system.

Brooks, T. R. (1995). Attitudes of medical students and family practice residents toward geriatric patients. Journal of the National Medical Association, 85, 61–64.

Coccaro, E. F., & Miles, A. M. (1984). The attitudinal impact of training in gerontology/geriatrics in medical school. Journal of the American Geriatrics Society, 32, 762–768.

Kosberg, J. J. (1983). The importance of attitudes on the interaction between health care providers and geriatric populations. In M. B. Kleiman (Ed.), Social gerontology (pp. 132–142). Basel: Karger.

Saarela, T., & Viukari, M. (1995). Attitudes of health care professionals towards care of the elderly. International Journal of Geriatric Psychiatry, 10, 797–800.

Williams, T. F. (1981). The physician viewpoint. In M. R. Haug (Ed.), Elderly patients and their doctors (pp. 42–46). New York: Springer.

Faith Healing

The search for alternative care outside of the traditional health care delivery system is an interesting topic suitable for lecture development. A discussion of faith healing can introduce a number of topics that are developed in later chapters (humanistic aspects of medical care, placebo effects, etc.). In addition, some studies indicate that faith healing may work in some instances (Chrisman & Kleinman, 1983; Jaffe, 1980), and in some ethnic groups the faith healer fulfills an important social role (Applewhite, 1995; Scott, 1974).

Applewhite, S. L., (1995). Curanderismo: Demystifying the health beliefs and practices of elderly Mexican Americans. Health and Social Work, 20, 247–253.

Chrisman, N. J., & Kleinman, A. (1983). Popular health care, social networks, and cultural meanings: The orientations of medical anthropology. In D. Mechanic (Ed.), Handbook of health, health care, and the health professions (pp. 569–590). New York: Free Press.

Jaffe, D. (1980). Healing from within. New York: Knopf.

Scott, C. S. (1974). Healing and health practices among five ethnic groups in Miami, Florida. Public Health Reports, 89, 524–532.

The Sick Role and Self-Enhancement

A recent study by Hamilton and Janata (1997) may be used to expand upon the text's discussion of the use of health services for nonmedical reasons. These researchers investigated Abnormal Illness Behavior (i.e., over-reporting or exaggerating of physical symptoms, preoccupation with illness, medical tests, and so forth) and put forth the argument that people with low self-esteem or identity problems engage in these behaviors in an effort to construct a positive sense of self.

Hamilton, J. C., & Janata, J. W. (1997). Dying to be ill: The role of self-enhancement motives in the spectrum of factitious disorders. Journal of Social and Clinical Psychology, 16, 178–199.

Exercises, Projects, and Activities

Providing Quality Health Care

Ask students to form four groups for a critical thinking exercise and team problem-solving assignments. Assign each group one of the projects outlined below. After discussing the problems and potential interventions in each scenario for approximately 30 minutes, have the groups report their findings to the class.

Project 1: You have been provided with state and federal funding to establish a comprehensive family practice clinic in the inner city. Describe your patients' profiles. What steps will you take to maximize patient use of this clinic?

Project 2: You are the administrative board of County General Hospital. The hospital has charged the board with the task of developing a program targeting delay behavior (e.g., seeking treatment for a suspected tumor). Describe educational and institutional interventions you might implement to minimize delay behavior.

Project 3: You are the administrative board of a private hospital that is committed to increasing patient satisfaction with care. Describe your patients' profiles. Describe the steps you might take to minimize depersonalization and to enhance patient perceptions of control.

Project 4: You are the administrative board of a pediatric hospital that is committed to increasing patient and parent satisfaction with care. Describe your patients' profiles. Describe the steps you might take to minimize depersonalization and to enhance patient perceptions of control.

Quackery

Discuss in class the factors that make patients susceptible to the influence of practitioners of medical fraud and quackery. Two examples that might stimulate classroom discussion are the overestimation of the prevalence of food allergies in children (Jarvis, 1993) and the assertation that cancer may be cured through sheer mental effort (Cassileth, 1990) A popular article by Don Colburn (1985) would make an excellent handout.

Cassileth, B. R. (1990). Mental health quackery in cancer treatment. International Journal of Mental Health, 19, 31–84.
 Colburn, D. (1985, June 19). Quackery. The Washington Post (pp. 10–12).
 Jarvis, W. T. (1993). Allergy-related quackery. New York State Journal of Medicine, 93, 100–104.

Recommended Reading

Maslach, C. (1982). Burnout: The cost of caring. Englewood Cliffs: Prentice-Hall.

The author presents a description of burnout, an overview of the personal and situational factors that accompany the syndrome, and its treatment.

Schaufeli, W. B., Maslach, C., & Marek, T. (Eds.). (1993). Professional burnout: Recent developments in theory and research. Washington, DC: Taylor & Francis.

This edited volume examines the phenomenon of burnout in a number of organizational contexts. It contains recent research investigating the nature of burnout, measurement issues, and addresses issues relevant to etiology and treatment.

True-False Questions

1. T   F   People's awareness of their internal physiological state is remarkably accurate. (ref. p. 238)

2. T   F   People who are anxious or neurotic are more likely to recognize physical symptoms and worry about them without seeking treatment. (ref. p. 239)

3. <u>T</u>   F   Highly prevalent risk factors or disorders are generally regarded as less serious than rare or distinctive risk factors or disorders. (ref. p. 241)

4. <u>T</u>   F   Symptoms that are painful are more likely to be interpreted as serious and requiring medical treatment. (ref. p. 241)

5. T   <u>F</u>   The role of psychological factors in the experience of symptoms is evidenced by the fact that women tend to minimize naturally fluctuating bodily states when they are premenstrual. (ref. p. 241)

6. T   <u>F</u>   As many as one in three American adults may use an unconventional therapy (e.g., homeopathy) during the course of a year. (ref. p. 244)

7. T   <u>F</u>   Although stress and emotional disorders are unrelated to physical symptoms, people use health services more during stressful times. (ref. p. 247)

8. <u>T</u>   F   Threats to self-esteem have been found to be related to the tendency to somaticize. (ref. p. 248)

9. <u>T</u>   F   Physicians are more likely to perceive female patients as psychologically disturbed. (ref. p. 248)

10. T   <u>F</u>   Once patients decide to see a doctor, the frequency of delay behavior is negligible. (ref. p. 252)

Multiple-Choice Questions

1. Symptom recognition is determined by individual differences in (ref. p. 239)
   <u>a</u>. attention to one's body and situational factors
   b. tolerance of physical symptoms and access to medical care
   c. physical reactivity and situational factors
   d. physical reactivity and cultural factors

2. Individual differences in neuroticism have been found to influence symptom (ref. p. 239)
   a. recognition but not reporting
   b. reporting but not recognition
   <u>c</u>. reporting and recognition
   d. none of the above

3. When under stress, people are more likely to (ref. p. 239)
   a. attribute stress-related physiological changes to stress rather than to illness
   <u>b</u>. attribute stress-related physiological changes to illness rather than to stress
   c. believe they are less vulnerable to illness and direct their attention outward
   d. repress their physical symptoms

4. People in a bad mood (ref. p. 240)
   a. suppress their symptoms and report fewer symptoms
   b. believe they are more capable of alleviating their symptoms
   <u>c</u>. are pessimistic that any actions they might take would relieve their symptoms
   d. perceive themselves as less vulnerable to future illness

5. Medical student's disease is an example of the role of _____ in the recognition of symptoms. (ref. p. 240)

   a. individual differences
   b. Type A behavior
   c. cultural differences
   d. situational factors

6. People who have a history of a particular medical condition (ref. p. 241)

   a. increase their vigilance and monitor their physical status to detect transitory changes in their bodily state
   b. increase their vigilance and seek out information about the condition in an attempt to regain mastery and control
   c. underestimate its prevalence in the general population and thus overestimate the threat to their health
   d. overestimate its prevalence in the general population and thus minimize the threat to their health

7. Illness schemas are acquired through (ref. p. 241)

   a. the media
   b. personal experience
   c. family and friends
   d. all of the above

8. One component of illness schemas involves perceptions of the range of symptoms and treatments associated with a particular disease. This component refers to the _____ of the disease. (ref. p. 242)

   a. identity
   b. consequences
   c. cure
   d. causes

9. Illness schemas develop in (ref. p. 242)

   a. childhood
   b. adolescence
   c. early adulthood
   d. middle age

10. Ruble (1972) found that women who believed they were premenstrual reported (ref. p. 242)

    a. fewer physiological and psychological symptoms
    b. more physiological symptoms but fewer psychological symptoms
    c. more physiological and psychological symptoms
    d. no changes in their physiological and psychological states

11. The _____ model of illness is represented by a long-term pattern of first few, then many, symptoms. (ref. pp. 242–243)

    a. acute
    b. chronic
    c. cyclic
    d. terminal

12. Disease prototypes influence people's (ref. p. 243)
    a. knowledge of their own disorders
    b. adherence to treatment regimens
    c. health-related behaviors
    d. all of the above

13. Bruce has found that he becomes increasingly fatigued after even mild exertion. He discusses his problem with his neighbor, Sam, who recently suffered from a similar problem. Sam tells him that a megadose of vitamin B complex completely eradicated his symptoms. Bruce tries Sam's remedy and does feel a little better. This is an example of (ref. p. 243)
    a. folk medicine
    b. self-care
    c. disease prototypes
    d. the lay referral network

14. The most accurate evaluation of the lay referral network is that it (ref. p. 244–245)
    a. always compromises patients' physical health
    b. makes formal medical care unnecessary
    c. has little impact on patients' health
    d. can be considered to complement the formal health care delivery system

15. The use of health services is lowest in (ref. p. 244)
    a. childhood
    b. adolescence and young adulthood
    c. middle age
    d. old age

16. Women are more likely than men to seek medical care. This may be due to (ref. p. 244)
    a. social norms that influence the expression of pain and symptoms
    b. women's relatively poor homeostatic mechanisms
    c. the comparatively greater economic costs women experience when they become ill
    d. all of the above

17. Compared to men, women's poor health may be attributed to (ref. p. 245)
    a. lower levels of employment
    b. higher rates of part-time employment
    c. lower economic status
    d. all of the above

18. The greatest social-class difference in the use of medical services is reflected in (ref. p. 246)
    a. budget cuts, which have restricted access to programs such as Medicare and Medicaid
    b. preventive health services
    c. the use of the lay referral network
    d. the use of emergency care services

19. The Health Belief Model best predicts the treatment-seeking behavior of (ref. p. 246)
    a. men
    b. women
    c. ethnic minorities
    d. people with money and access to health services

20. The patient who complains of a medical disorder that is rightfully psychological in nature is more likely to be treated by a (ref. p. 247)
    a. psychiatrist
    b. general practitioner
    c. specialist
    d. lay practitioner

21. Doctors treat a very large proportion of their patients for disorders that are psychological in origin due to the fact that (ref. p. 247)
    a. patients must recognize and interpret physical symptoms
    b. anxiety and depression often are accompanied by physical symptoms
    c. patients with psychological problems may be stigmatized by others
    d. all of the above

22. Somaticizers (ref. p. 248)
    a. exhibit strong beliefs in self-care
    b. tend to express distress and conflict through physical symptoms
    c. repress their symptoms during times of stress
    d. all of the above

23. The notion that illness may actually be reinforcing because it exempts the individual from daily responsibilities is termed (ref. p. 248)
    a. malingering
    b. delay behavior
    c. secondary gains
    d. hypochondriasis

24. Illness delay is the time (ref. p. 250)
    a. it takes an individual to decide that a symptom is serious
    b. between the recognition that a symptom implies an illness and the decision to seek treatment
    c. between deciding to seek treatment and actually doing so
    d. between a person's recognition of a symptom and when the person seeks treatment

25. The correct order of the stages of delay in seeking treatment is (ref. p. 250)
    a. appraisal, illness, behavioral, and medical delay
    b. behavioral, appraisal, illness, and medical delay
    c. appraisal, illness, medical, and behavioral delay
    d. appraisal, symptom, illness, and medical delay

26. Time spent in the emergency room may be thought of as a function of (ref. p. 250)
    a. appraisal delay
    b. illness delay
    c. symptom delay
    d. medical delay

27. Delay is most common among people who (ref. p. 250)
    a. have an internal locus of control and value self-care
    b. are elderly and who perceive their symptoms to be serious
    c. have no regular contact with a physician
    d. have a poor interpersonal relationship with their regular physician

28. The nature of physical symptoms may play an important role in a patient's delay behavior. Specifically, a patient will seek treatment less quickly when a symptom (ref. p. 252)
    a. is new
    b. is highly visible
    c. does not hurt
    d. none of the above

29. Medical delay (ref. p. 252)
    a. accounts for at least 30% of all delay behaviors
    b. is more likely when symptoms deviate from the practitioner's disease prototype
    c. is more likely in cases where the diagnosis is not serious
    d. is unrelated to the diagnostic process

30. You have been asked to develop a public information program designed to minimize the delay behavior of people who evidence one or more of the seven warning signs of cancer. Considering the research evidence presented in your text, the most effective appeal would emphasize the fact that (ref. pp. 250–252)
    a. certain cancers have a very poor prognosis and high mortality rate
    b. although the side effects can be debilitating, chemotherapy and radiation therapy can successfully treat many cancers
    c. aggressive treatment enhances one's chances of surviving cancer
    d. precancerous symptoms are seldom troublesome or alarming, yet everyone is vulnerable to the disease and should seek early treatment

31. The role of the hospital has changed significantly over the last few decades. As hospitals have assumed many treatment functions, hospital admissions have _____ and the average length of hospitalization has _____ . (ref. p. 253)
    a. decreased; increased
    b. increased; decreased
    c. leveled off; decreased
    d. leveled off; increased

32. The hospital nursing staff has as its primary orientation the goal of (ref. p. 254)
    a. cure
    b. care
    c. core
    d. all of the above

33. Status distinctions among hospital staff are frequently reflected in social interaction and communication patterns. A study of nosocomial infection (Raven, Freeman, & Haley, 1982) revealed that (ref. p. 255)

   a. physicians served as positive role models to other physicians, but nurses were unlikely to comment on physicians' conduct

   b. administrators reported that they would hesitate to correct a physician but would frequently correct the nursing staff

   c. physicians were concerned about the conduct of the nursing staff, but they felt that even constructive comments would further exacerbate problems of burnout

   <u>d</u>. communication was poor across each of the different levels of the hospital hierarchy

34. Which of the following is **not** one of the three components of burnout? (ref. p. 256)

   a. emotional exhaustion

   <u>b</u>. derogation of the client

   c. depersonalization of the client

   d. reduced sense of personal accomplishment

35. Burnout may result from (ref. p. 256)

   <u>a</u>. the need to provide services for a person who may not be helped

   b. high rates of absenteeism and job turnover

   c. the need to curb one's feelings of empathy

   d. all of the above

36. Hector has worked as an RN in the pediatrics ward at County General Hospital for the past 3 years. He has been experiencing increasing levels of stress over the last 3 months due to a number of changes in his department. Hospital administrators have been pressuring the nursing staff to increase the number of patients for whom they are responsible. On the other hand, Hector feels that a number of his younger patients need a substantial amount of individualized care. Hector is suffering from (ref. p. 255)

   a. burnout

   b. role ambiguity

   <u>c</u>. role conflict

   d. objectivity

37. Shinn et al. (1984) found that people who show few symptoms of burnout (ref. p. 257)

   a. have effective coping styles

   <u>b</u>. habitually turn to others for help

   c. protect themselves by becoming emotionally detached from their work

   d. have hardy, optimistic personalities

38. Attempts to contain costs by the creation of diagnostic-related groups (DRGs) have resulted in pressure on hospitals (ref. p. 256)

   a. from third-party reimbursement programs to cut patient stays and treatment costs

   b. to establish increasingly homogenized standards of clinical treatment and hospitalization

   c. to admit more patients for shorter stays

   <u>d</u>. all of the above

39. "Good" patients (ref. p. 259)
    a. take an active role in their health care
    b. are better adjusted and are more satisfied with their medical care
    c. assume a passive role and may become helpless and dependent
    d. have shorter recovery times than problem patients

40. Patients may react to a loss of personal control by developing (ref. pp. 259–260)
    a. helplessness
    b. reactance
    c. anxiety and depression
    d. all of the above

41. According to Taylor (1979), the loss of control experienced by a patient affects his or her (ref. pp. 259–260)
    a. interpersonal interactions with the medical staff but not the quality of the medical care received
    b. interpersonal behavior, physiological responses, and psychological state
    c. psychological state, behavior, and interpersonal style
    d. none of the above

42. Studies of the effects of presurgical control-enhancing interventions suggest that (ref. pp. 260–261)
    a. a moderate level of fear and the work of worrying is essential to good postoperative adjustment
    b. providing preoperative training has a beneficial effect on patients' physical and emotional adjustment
    c. providing preoperative training has a beneficial effect on patients' physical, but not emotional, adjustment
    d. while providing preoperative training is associated with good postoperative adjustment, cognitive reappraisal training has little effect

43. The results of research evaluating control-enhancing interventions utilized with stressful medical procedures suggests that patient coping is facilitated by (ref. p. 262)
    a. information about the procedure
    b. cognitive-behavioral interventions
    c. relaxation training
    d. all of the above

44. Enhancing a patient's sense of personal control may be (ref. p. 263)
    a. aversive if it gives him or her more responsibility than is tolerable
    b. especially beneficial for patients who are high in desire for control
    c. stressful if it involves too many choices or too much information
    d. all of the above

45. Children's adverse reactions to hospitalization may be attributable to (ref. pp. 263–264)
    a. separation anxiety
    b. lack of information about medical procedures
    c. high levels of personal control
    d. all of the above

Essay Questions

1. Explain how social and psychological factors are implicated in the recognition and interpretation of symptoms. (ref. pp. 239–241)

2. How prevalent is the utilization of health care services for nonmedical complaints? Who is likely to do so and why? (ref. pp. 247–248)

3. Explain how hospitalization may affect patients' sense of personal control. What reactions are commonly observed? (ref. pp. 258–260)

4. Summarize the research investigating the effectiveness of control-enhancing interventions. (ref. pp. 260–263)

5. Your brother calls to inform you that his 9-year-old son is being hospitalized. Based upon the research in the text, what advice would you give him to minimize any adverse reactions that your nephew might experience? (ref. pp. 264–266)

Chapter Outline

F.	Situational Determinants of Placebo Effects
G.	Social Norms and Placebo Effects
H.	Generalizability of Placebo Effects
I.	The Placebo as a Methodological Tool

Learning Objectives

1. Describe trends in the changing roles of health providers, including nurse-practitioners and physician assistants.

2. Describe the criteria by which patients judge the adequacy of their medical care.

3. Describe factors inherent in the medical setting that influence the quality of patient-provider communication.

4. Describe factors inherent in the structure of the health care delivery system that influence the quality of patient-provider communication.

5. Compare and contrast the characteristics of private, fee-for-service care and health maintenance organizations.

6. Describe the changes in the philosophy of health care delivery in the United States.

7. Describe providers' behaviors that contribute to faulty patient-provider communication.

8. Describe patient factors that contribute to faulty patient-provider communication.

9. Describe qualities of the provider-patient interaction that contribute to faulty communication.

10. Describe the prevalence and assessment of nonadherence to treatment regimens.

11. Describe the causes of nonadherence to treatment regimens.

12. Define creative nonadherence and the factors that contribute to creative nonadherence to treatment regimens.

13. Explain the role of reactance and self-labeling to nonadherence to treatment regimens.

14. Explain the relationship of patient-provider communication to malpractice litigation.

15. Describe the nature and effectiveness of interventions designed to teach providers how to communicate effectively with patients.

16. Describe the nature and effectiveness of strategies for improving patient adherence to treatment regimens.

17. Trace the use of placebos from the early days of medicine to the present day.

18. Define placebo, and describe the nature of the placebo effect and its role in medical treatment.

19. Describe how the effectiveness of the placebo effect may be influenced by provider behaviors.

20. Describe how the effectiveness of the placebo effect may be influenced by patient characteristics.

21. Describe how the effectiveness of the placebo effect may be influenced by patient-provider communication.

22. Describe situational determinants of the placebo effect.

23. Describe how the effectiveness of the placebo effect may be influenced by social norms.

24. Describe the generalizability of the placebo effect.

25. Explain how the placebo may be used as a methodological tool.

Lecture Suggestions

Nonverbal Behavior Within the Medical Interaction

The nonverbal behavior exchanged between patients and their providers may be a revealing source of information about interpersonal expectations and attitudes. For example, patients often complain about being treated in a patronizing or dehumanizing fashion by medical providers. Caporael and her colleagues (Caporael, Lukaszewski, & Culbertson, 1983; Culbertson & Caporael, 1983) reported that a high frequency of "baby talk" (i.e., short, simplistic sentences) was being directed toward institutionalized elderly patients by their caregivers. They generally found that patients disliked being addressed in this fashion (the only exceptions were the patients who suffered from cognitive impairment). In addition, they concluded that this linguistic register conveyed an expectation of helplessness and dependency to the patient. These findings might be discussed in conjunction with the problems of adherence, the depersonalization associated with institutionalization, perceptions of control, patient satisfaction, and the issue of medical ageism introduced in Chapter 9 of this manual.

Caporael, L. R., Lukaszewski, M. P., & Culbertson, G. H. (1983). Secondary baby talk: Judgments by institutionalized elderly and their caregivers. Journal of Personality and Social Psychology, 44, 746–754.
Culbertson, G. H., & Caporael, L. R. (1983). Baby talk speech to the elderly. Complexity and content of messages. Personality and Social Psychology Bulletin, 9, 305–312.

Medical Training and Providers' Attitudes

The process of attitude change and socialization in medical training has received a great deal of attention. Critics argue that the rigors of medical school promote a sense of emotional detachment and cynicism among students. A number of sociological and psychological analyses (e. g., Becker & Geer, 1985; Becker, Geer, Hughes, & Strauss, 1961; Campbell, 1973; Shapiro & Lowenstein, 1979) of the process of medical school socialization are readily available and may provide instructors with a range of sources of supplementary lecture material.

Becker, H. S., & Geer, B. (1985). The fate of idealism in medical school. <u>American Sociological Review</u>, <u>23</u>, 50–56.

Becker, H. S., Geer, B., Hughes, E. C., & Strauss, A. L. (1961). <u>Boys in white: Student culture in medical school</u>. Chicago: University of Chicago Press.

Campbell, M. A. (1973). <u>Why would a girl go into medicine</u>? Westbury: The Feminist Press.

Shapiro, E. C., & Lowenstein, L. M. (Eds.). (1979). <u>Becoming a physician</u>. Cambridge: Ballinger.

Ethics and the Use of Placebos

The text's discussion of placebo effects may be supplemented by a lecture that addresses the ethical uses of placebos within the experimental and therapeutic context. Rawlinson (1985) raises issues of paternalism within the provider-patient interaction, and Fink (1985) and Lieberman (1996) discuss the general ethical issues surrounding the use of placebos.

Fink, M. (1985). Discussion: The ethics of placebo. In L. White, B. Tursky, & G. E. Schwartz (Eds.), <u>Placebo: Theory, research and mechanisms</u>. New York: Guilford.

Lieberman, J. A. (1996). Ethical dilemmas in clinical research with human subjects: An investigator's perspective. <u>Psychopharmacology Bulletin</u>, 32, 19–25.

Rawlinson, M. C. (1985). Truth-telling and paternalism in the clinic: Philosophical reflections on the use of placebos in medical practice. In L. White, B. Tursky, & G. E. Schwartz (Eds.), <u>Placebo: Theory, research and mechanisms</u>. New York: Guilford.

Exercises, Projects, and Activities

Evaluation of Student Health Center

If you have the support of the campus student health center director, an evaluation of the facility's psychosocial climate makes a useful class assignment. I have found that campus health care personnel will make their facilities open for individual student tours during a specified time block. This assignment takes some advance planning, but student responses have been very positive. It is important for students to understand that patients' privacy must be respected, and that they must follow any guidelines that the health care personnel may provide. Assignments might follow the outline below.

The Director of Student Health has agreed to make the on-campus facilities available to the class to evaluate the psychosocial environment in the center. In order to protect patient confidentiality, it is important that you do not conduct your evaluation during the times that they have physicians examining patients. Typically, these times are as follows:

1. Monday through Friday, 4:00 to 4:30 p.m.

2. Tuesday, Wednesday, Friday, 12:00 to 2:00 p.m.

3. Monday and Thursday, 7:30 to 9:30 a.m.

Your assignment should follow these guidelines:

1. Develop a system of evaluating the clinic's psychosocial climate (include your criteria and questions with your assignment).

2. Conduct an evaluation of the clinic according to your criteria.

3. What do you conclude about the psychosocial environment? Do you have any recommendations for improvement? If so, what are they?

Recommended Reading

DiMatteo, M. R., & DiNicola, D. D. (1982). <u>Achieving patient compliance.</u> Elmsford: Pergamon.

This volume provides a psychosocial analysis of the problem of patient compliance from within the framework of the patient-provider interaction. Topics include the quality of communication and interpersonal issues within the medical interaction, characteristics of patients, normative issues, beliefs, and attitudes.

Spiro, H. M., Curnen, M. G. M., Peschel, E., & St. James, D. (Eds.). (1993). <u>Empathy and the practice of medicine: Beyond pills and the scalpel.</u> New Haven, CT: Yale University Press.

This edited volume addresses the role of empathy in humanistic medical training programs. Chapters address topics such as the nature of empathy, techniques to teach empathy to premedical and medical students, and the role of emotion in the practice of medicine.

True-False Questions

1. T **F** Physicians' assistants typically have completed more than the typical 2 to 4 years of basic nursing education. (ref. p. 269)

2. T **F** Because of the changes in the roles of allied health professions (such as nurse-practitioners and physicians' assistants), it is likely that future health care will be associated with increased status differentials between health care providers. (ref. p. 269)

3. **T** F DRGs have had a significant effect on modern medical care in that they encourage the early detection and treatment of medical complications. (ref. p. 272)

4. **T** F The changing philosophy of health care delivery means that many physicians recognize that there are less intrusive alternatives to traditional medical management. (ref. p. 274)

5. T **F** A study by Hall et al. (1993) found that male and female physicians preferred female patients. (ref. p. 278)

6. T **F** Estimates of nonadherence vary from a low of 50% to over 90%. (ref. p. 281)

7. **T** F Malpractice litigation has become more common as medicine becomes more complex. (ref. pp. 286–287)

8. **T** F Patients are remarkably good at predicting their adherence to treatment regimens. (ref. p. 290)

9. **T** F Adherence to treatment is substantially increased when the provider is able to draw on their personal authority as well as the power of medical authority. (ref. p. 290)

10.   T   **F**   The placebo effect is solely due to psychological expectations of improved health and alleviation of symptoms. (ref. p. 293)

Multiple-Choice Questions

1.   Rita is trained in traditional nursing and also has received special training in primary care. She is affiliated with a group of private practice physicians, sees her own patients, and provides routine medical care, prescribes treatment, and attends to chronically ill and walk-in patients with a myriad of disorders. Rita is a(n) (ref. p. 268)

   a.   advanced practice nurse

   <u>b.</u>   nurse-practitioner

   c.   physician's assistant

   d.   clinical nurse specialist

2.   Most patients (ref. p. 270)

   a.   are good judges of the technical quality of the medical care they receive

   <u>b.</u>   consider medical treatment to be successful if their symptoms improve

   c.   feel that the technical quality of medical care is somewhat more important than the manner in which it is provided

   d.   all of the above

3.   Patient satisfaction is highest when the provider (ref. p. 270)

   a.   is technically competent

   b.   has a degree from a prestigious institution

   c.   expresses concern and uncertainty about the patient's condition

   <u>d.</u>   is interpersonally warm and confident

4.   The technical quality of medical care and the manner in which it is provided are (ref. p. 270)

   a.   critical determinants of patient satisfaction

   b.   important factors in the prevalence of malpractice litigation

   c.   important factors in doctor shopping

   <u>d.</u>   unrelated

5.   A network of affiliated providers who have agreed to charge preestablished rates for particular services is termed a (ref. p. 271)

   a.   health maintenance organization (HMO)

   <u>b.</u>   preferred provider organization (PPO)

   c.   diagnostic related group (DRG)

   d.   quality circle (QC)

6.   A colleague orientation is most likely to develop (ref. p. 272)

   a.   when providers include their patients as active partners in their health and medical care

   <u>b.</u>   among providers affiliated with a prepaid health care plan

   c.   among private providers who are paid directly for fee-for-service care

   d.   among providers who are committed to providing a high quality of technical care

7. A survey by Ware et al. (1996) revealed that patient care was highest in (ref. p. 345)

   a. private fee-for-service practices

   b. HMOs

   c. PPOs

   d. large medical practices

8. You are a consultant who has been hired by an HMO to try to improve patient satisfaction and retention. Based on the research discussed in the text, your most effective recommendation would be to (ref. p. 272)

   a. increase the number of specialists

   b. allow patients more personal choice in their primary provider

   c. decrease the annual premium paid

   d. ensure that a patient sees a different doctor during each visit

9. According to the text, one of the changes in the philosophy of health care delivery that affects patient-provider relationships is (ref. p. 274)

   a. Western medicine's resistance to nontraditional therapies such as meditation and biofeedback

   b. in response to increased consumerism among patients, medical students become less egalitarian in their relationships with patients during the course of medical training

   c. provider-patient relationships are becoming more egalitarian

   d. none of the above

10. The status differences inherent between traditional providers and their patients may be reflected in (ref. pp. 275–276)

    a. the active involvement of patients with their treatment regimens

    b. the use of jargon or baby talk

    c. the manner in which patients interrupt medical providers

    d. the provider's overestimation of the level of patients' technical understanding

11. According to a study by McKinlay (1975), providers (ref. p. 276)

    a. accurately report that patients' knowledge of medical terms is quite low

    b. underestimate the level of their patients' understanding of medical terms

    c. overestimate the level of their patients' understanding of medical terms

    d. tend to blame themselves for their patients' lack of knowledge of medical terms

12. Patient depersonalization (ref. p. 277)

    a. serves no valid medical function

    b. is disturbing to patients but has little effect on the quality of the patient-provider relationship

    c. is disturbing to patients but has no adverse medical effects

    d. can provide emotional protection to the provider

13. The affect communicated by a physician in interaction with a patient can have a substantial impact on the patient's (ref. p. 277)

    a. attitude toward the physician

    b. attitude toward the visit

    c. medical condition

    d. all of the above

14. Providers have more positive attitudes toward (ref. p. 278)

   a. Black or Hispanic patients

   b. acutely ill patients

   c. sicker patients

   d. patients with psychological disorders

15. In Wilcox's (1992) study of attitudes toward male and female patients, female patients were perceived to be more likely to (ref. p. 278)

   a. be seriously ill

   b. require follow-up tests

   c. require a nonpsychiatric consultation

   d. be recommended for medication

16. The extent of faulty provider-patient communication on patient retention of information is reflected in the fact that up to _____ cannot repeat their diagnosis and up to _____ do not understand important details of their illness or treatment. (ref. p. 279)

   a. one-half; three-quarters

   b. one-third; one-half

   c. one-half; one-third

   d. one-third; three-quarters

17. Patients (ref. pp. 279–280)

   a. often respond to different cues than do providers and also provide faulty cues about their true concerns

   b. are more concerned with their underlying illness than its symptoms than are providers

   c. present their most distressing symptoms clearly and precisely; most faulty communication occurs with minor symptoms

   d. have little difficulty interpreting and reporting their symptoms

18. Qualities of the medical interaction that exacerbate communication problems include the fact that (ref. pp. 280–281)

   a. providers receive little feedback from their patients

   b. patients are more likely to provide negative rather than positive feedback

   c. patients seldom provide feedback about the effectiveness of providers' communication

   d. all of the above

19. Dissatisfied patients are more likely to (ref. p. 281)

   a. seek treatment that meets their emotional rather than medical needs

   b. use medical services in the future and thus be accused of malingering

   c. seek more technically competent medical treatment

   d. schedule frequent medical checkups

20. When patients do not adopt the recommended medical treatment, the result is (ref. p. 281)
    a. malingering
    b. reactance
    c. doctor shopping
    d. nonadherence

21. For short-term antibiotic regimens, an estimated _____ fail to comply adequately. (ref. p. 281)
    a. one-quarter
    b. one-third
    c. one-fifth
    d. three-quarters

22. For the most part, physicians' estimates of their patients' rates of adherence are (ref. p. 282)
    a. accurate
    b. artificially high
    c. artificially low
    d. reliable

23. The greatest cause of nonadherence to treatment is (ref. p. 282)
    a. the patient's unsupportive home environment
    b. the patient's uncooperative personality
    c. faulty patient-provider communication
    d. the decreasing use of traditional health plans

24. Adherence is higher in patients who are (ref. pp. 282–283)
    a. anxious and vigilant
    b. satisfied with their provider
    c. younger, white, and female
    d. asked to change personal habits

25. Which of the following medical suggestions would be **most** likely to show high rates of nonadherence? (ref. pp. 283)
    a. "Take three tablets per day for five days."
    b. "Please stop by the lab on your way out and have some blood drawn for a complete battery."
    c "Make sure you schedule a mammogram before your next appointment."
    d. "Try to rest and take some annual leave from your job."

26. Overall adherence rates are poorest (ref. pp. 283)
    a. when patients must change personal habits
    b. with complex self-care regimens
    c. when the advice is perceived as medical
    d. when the treatment seems nonmedical

27. Avoidant coping strategies on the part of patients are (ref. pp. 284–285)
    a. associated with good adherence to treatment regimens
    b. associated with poor adherence to treatment regimens
    c. associated with creative nonadherence
    d. unrelated with adherence to treatment regimens
28. Creative nonadherence (ref. p. 285)
    a. seriously undermines a patient's health
    b. is unrelated to disease prototypes
    c. may be either intentional or accidental
    d. all of the above
29. The psychological state that results when people feel that their freedoms have been arbitrarily restricted by some external factor or agent is termed (ref. p. 285)
    a. reactance
    b. learned helplessness
    c. depression
    d. self-efficacy
30. Which of the following encourages adherence to treatment regimens? (ref. p. 287)
    a. social support
    b. education
    c. anxiety
    d. general attitudes toward medical care
31. A physician's "bedside manner" (ref. p. 288)
    a. is an art and is not significantly affected by learning
    b. can be improved through teaching more effective communication skills
    c. has little effect on his or her technical competence
    d. has little effect on the prevalence of malpractice litigation
32. The best predictor of physician sensitivity is (ref. p. 288)
    a. extraversion
    b. technical competence
    c. an interest in people
    d. idealism
33. Communication-skills training for physicians should include (ref. pp. 288–289)
    a. a consideration of the limitations and demands of the medical setting
    b. the effective use of nonverbal behaviors
    c. the effective exchange of information
    d. all of the above

34. According to a study of patient-provider communication skills conducted by Thompson, Nanni, and Schwankovsky (1990), patient satisfaction, perceptions of personal control, and patient question-asking was highest in (ref. p. 289)

   a. women who listed questions before the visit

   b. women whose physicians encouraged the asking of questions

   c. women who listed questions before the visit and women whose physicians encouraged the asking of questions

   d. none of the above

35. Most physicians today (ref. p. 290)

   a. have received training in health promotion and health-habit modification

   b. have received little formal training in health promotion yet feel that health promotion and health-habit modification play important roles in patients' health and medical care

   c. feel that they are the most effective agents for the provision of effective health promotion

   d. none of the above

36. Adherence to treatment is improved when providers (ref. p. 290)

   a. provide written instructions about treatment, dosage, and side effects

   b. ask patients about potential barriers to adherence

   c. make use of their personal authority

   d. all of the above

37. Research on the effectiveness of incentives on keeping appointments indicate that (ref. p. 290)

   a. incentives are not a cost-effective way to improve appointment-keeping

   b. incentives are a reliable way to improve appointment-keeping

   c. once incentives are removed, patients may show worsened adherence

   d. incentives have no effect upon appointment-keeping

38. Effective training in communication skills must focus on providers' (ref. p. 291)

   a. emotional expressivity

   b. clear and effective exchange of information

   c. listening skills

   d. all of the above

39. John has asked his friend, Joe, to refer him to a good family provider. Joe suggests that he make an appointment with his own physician, Dr. Smith. Joe says, "Dr. Smith is a wonderful physician--she really cares about me as a person." In this case, Dr. Smith has developed (ref. p. 292)

   a. legitimate power

   b. referent power

   c. personal authority

   d. all of the above

40. The placebo effect (ref. pp. 292–294)
    a. accounted for much of the success of early medical treatments but is seldom an important aspect of modern medical care
    b. accounts for improvements in the patient's psychological state but is unrelated to actual physiological changes
    c. has been observed in both patients and providers
    d. is powerful but of short duration

41. Placebo effects may be associated with (ref. pp. 294–295)
    a. improvements in patients' medical conditions
    b. reductions in patients' anxiety
    c. increased release of endorphins
    d. all of the above

42. Placebo effects vary according to (ref. p. 294–295)
    a. how a provider interacts with the patient
    b. how much a provider believes in the power of the placebo
    c. a provider's warmth, confidence, and empathy
    d. all of the above

43. Stronger placebo effects have been observed in patients who are high in (ref. p. 295)
    a. need for approval
    b. self-esteem
    c. internal orientation
    d. all of the above

44. Which of the following instructions would produce the strongest placebo effect? (ref. pp. 295–296)
    a. "Take two of these [sugar] pills every four hours."
    b. "Eat more complex carbohydrates and less fats."
    c. "Get more rest, and you might want to take an occasional multivitamin when you feel fatigued."
    d. "Take one of these whenever you feel discomfort."

45. The presence of a placebo effect is reflected in the importance placed by the medical community on (ref. p. 297)
    a. double-blind studies
    b. prospective studies
    c. retrospective studies
    d. drug studies

Essay Questions

1. How have recent changes in the American health care delivery system affected the provider-patient relationship? (ref. pp. 269–275)

2. Explain how attributes of both patients and their health care providers contribute to faulty communication in the medical setting. (ref. pp. 275–281)

3. Explain the ways in which interventions that target health care providers' communication skills may be related to increased patient satisfaction and increased adherence. (ref. pp. 288–292)

4. A friend is laughing about a friend's self-prescribed herbal remedies. He scoffs that the placebo effect is purely psychological, thus "all in your head." Explain the nature and effect of placebos, and why this statement is inaccurate. (ref. pp. 293–294)

5. Explain how health care providers might use the placebo effect to its best advantage. (ref. pp. 294–296)

CHAPTER 10
PAIN AND ITS MANAGEMENT

Chapter Outline

I.   Significance of Pain

II.   Elusive Nature of Pain

      A.   Measuring Pain

      B.   Physiology of Pain

            1.   History

            2.   Overview

      C.   Gate Theory of Pain

      D.   Neurochemical Bases of Pain and Its Inhibition

III.   Clinical Management of Pain

      A.   Acute Versus Chronic Pain

      B.   Pain and Personality

IV.   Pain Control Techniques

      A.   Pharmacological Control of Pain

      B.   Surgical Control of Pain

      C.   Sensory Control of Pain

      D.   Biofeedback

      E.   Relaxation Techniques

      F.   Hypnosis

      G.   Acupuncture

      H.   Distraction

      I.   Coping Techniques

      J.   Guided Imagery

      K.   Additional Cognitive Techniques to Control Pain

V.   Management of Chronic Pain

      A.   Pain Management Programs

Learning Objectives

1. Explain the medical and psychological significance of pain.

2. Explain the role of the social context in the experience of pain.

3. Describe the techniques of pain measurement.

4. Explain the physiological aspects of pain.

5. Describe the gate theory of pain.

6. Describe the neurochemical bases of pain and pain inhibition.

7. Compare and contrast acute and chronic pain. Define the different kinds of chronic pain (i.e., chronic benign pain, recurrent acute pain, and chronic progressive pain).

8. Describe the psychological and social consequences of chronic pain.

9. Describe the relationship between individual differences in personality and the experience of chronic and acute pain.

10. Describe pharmacological techniques to control pain and their effectiveness.

11. Describe surgical techniques to control pain and their effectiveness.

12. Describe the use of counterirritation as a sensory method of pain control and its effectiveness.

13. Describe the use of biofeedback to control pain and its effectiveness.

14. Describe the use of relaxation techniques to control pain and their effectiveness.

15. Describe the use of hypnosis to control pain and its effectiveness.

16. Describe the use of acupuncture to control pain and its effectiveness.

17. Describe the use of distraction to control pain and its effectiveness.

18. Describe the use of coping techniques to control pain and their effectiveness.

19. Describe the use of guided imagery to control pain and its effectiveness.

20. Describe the use of cognitive techniques to control pain and their effectiveness.

21. Explain the principles of chronic pain management.

22. Describe the nature of pain management programs.

Lecture Suggestions

Migraine

      Many students are familiar with the pain of migraine headaches, and this topic might be an interesting way to introduce this chapter. MacGregor (1997) presents an interesting discussion of the diagnosis and treatment of migraine, with a focus on problems of adherence. Solomon (1997) discusses pain assessment with an emphasis on functional status and quality of life.

MacGregor, E. A. (1997). The doctor and the migraine patient: Improving compliance. Neurology, 48, S16–S20.

Solomon, G. D. (1997). Evolution of the measurement of quality of life in migraine. Neurology, 48, S10–S15.

Chronic Pain as a Self-Handicapping Strategy

The experience of chronic pain may have a profound influence on one's self-image. Elton, Stanley, and Burrows (1978) found that chronic pain patients suffer from low self-esteem. On the other hand, chronic pain may serve a self-protective function if it permits the patient to engage in a self-handicapping strategy. Mayerson and Rhodewalt (1988) found that subjects with low self-esteem reported higher pain ratings under experimental conditions (i. e., immersion of the hand in ice water) and were more likely to attribute greater performance impairment to their perceived pain. They conclude that a potential self-serving function of pain-related attributions must be considered when designing pain intervention programs.

Elton, D., Stanley, G. V., & Burrows, G. D. (1978). Self-esteem and chronic pain. Journal of Psychosomatic Research, 22, 25–30.

Mayerson, N. H., & Rhodewalt, F. (1988). Role of self-protective attributions in the experience of pain. Journal of Social and Clinical Psychology, 6, 203–218.

Exercises, Projects, and Activities

Pain Management Programs

If your university is affiliated with a medical center or if a local rehabilitation clinic is accessible, request a guest speaker for a classroom presentation of pain management intervention techniques.

The Subjective Experience of Pain

Have students write essays about an incident during which their experience of pain was modulated by some set of psychological or situational factors. With some thought, most students can recall a sports-related injury or a stressful experience that influenced their perception of pain. A sample assignment might follow these guidelines.

The readings and the material discussed during this week of class focus on the experience of pain and techniques by which individuals and/or providers manage their physical pain. Pick any topic discussed in class or in this week's readings and write a brief essay on this topic. Your essay should include:

1. a brief description of a personal experience or an observation that illustrates one or more of the phenomena covered in class or the text;

2. a brief explanation of the theory or research which you will apply to this experience or observation; and

3. an evaluation of how well this research or theory seems to explain this experience or observation.

Medical/Dental Procedures and Pain Management

An alternative assignment might involve specifically targeting the control of pain and anxiety during a medical or dental procedure. The use of an interview format would ensure that students assess the perception of pain in a comprehensive and thorough manner. A sample assignment is provided below.

Interview two friends (use pseudonyms, please) and ask them to recall a medical or dental procedure during which they had to regulate the amount of pain and/or anxiety they were experiencing. Then, analyze your friends' responses within the context of the issues discussed in Chapter 10 of the text and lectures. This task will consist of the following:

1. Develop a brief interview format which you will use to discuss these issues. Make it specific in order to address the goals of this assignment. Include your interview format as an appendix to your assignment.

2. Discuss the specific interview responses in relationship to pain and its control and management.

3. What do you conclude about your friends' experiences with pain and its management? What factors seem to be involved in successful pain control and management (if observed)? Can you identify factors that seem to explain why your friends might have had difficulty managing their pain?

4. What role (if any) did perceived control play?

5. Make sure you incorporate the theories and concepts discussed in class in your analysis.

Recommended Reading

Barber, J., & Adrian, C. (Eds.). (1982). Psychological approaches to the management of pain. New York: Brunner/Mazel.

This volume contains chapters related to the diagnosis, evaluation, and rehabilitation of chronic and acute pain.

Melzack, R., & Wall, P. D. (1982). The challenge of pain. New York: Basic Books.

This classic study of pain reviews theories of pain, the underlying physiological elements of pain, and techniques of pain management and control.

Skevington, S. M. (1995). Psychology of pain. New York: Wiley.

This text provides an overview of pain research for advanced students and professionals. The author reviews biological mechanisms, measurement, and theories of pain. Also discussed are variables such as gender, personal control, and coping that influence the perception of pain.

Turk, D. C., Meichenbaum, D., & Genest, M. (1983). Pain and behavioral medicine: A cognitive-behavioral perspective. New York: Guilford.

Written for professionals and advanced students, this volume describes therapeutic techniques, studies of acute and chronic pain, psychological factors in the experience of pain, and the treatment components of a comprehensive pain management program.

True-False Questions

1. T   F   There is a strong positive correlation between perceived pain and severity of symptoms. (ref. p. 300)

2.   T   _F_   Zborowski (1958) has found ethnic differences in the ability to discriminate painful stimuli. (ref. p. 301)

3.   T   _F_   The McGill Pain Questionnaire assesses pain behaviors. (ref. p. 301)

4.   _T_   F   Evaluations of the specificity and pattern theories of pain suggest that specialized fibers do conduct pain, but that patterns of stimulation also are important. (ref. p. 305)

5.   T   _F_   Beta-endorphins produce peptides that have widespread neuronal, endocrine, and central nervous system distributions. (ref. p. 308)

6.   T   _F_   Chronic pain is a sufficient condition for the development of depression. (ref. p. 313)

7.   _T_   F   Psychological pain management techniques are most effective in managing slow-rising pains. (ref. p. 316)

8.   T   _F_   Hypnosis is the most commonly used strategy for the management and treatment of acute and chronic pain. (ref. p. 319)

9.   _T_   F   Acupuncture may trigger the release of endorphins, thus reducing the experience of pain. (ref. p. 320)

10.   _T_   F   Most chronic pain management programs provide outpatient treatment. (ref. p. 324)

Multiple-Choice Questions

1.   Pain (ref. p. 300)
    a.   is directly related to the severity of physical symptoms
    _b._   has an important survival function
    c.   has little medical significance outside of motivating most patients to seek treatment
    d.   is an important component of most medical school curricula

2.   Pain has important medical consequences because (ref. p. 300)
    a.   patients' delay behavior is related to the experience of debilitating pain
    b.   practitioners are trained to devote a significant amount of time to diagnosing the source of pain, and this frequently impairs the quality of medical interactions
    _c._   the practitioner focuses attention on symptoms that may have more medical significance, and the patient feels an important problem is neglected
    d.   after death, pain is the most feared aspect of illness or medical treatment

3.   Pain is (ref. p. 301)
    _a._   a subjective experience
    b.   relatively easy to measure
    c.   of little functional value
    d.   a sensory experience

4. Beecher's (1959) study of wartime injuries investigated the effect of _____ on pain. (ref. p. 301)

    a. placebos
    b. fear
    c. arousal
    d. interpretation

5. Cross-cultural differences have been found in the (ref. p. 301)

    a. discrimination of painful stimuli
    b. reporting and intensity of reactions to pain
    c. sensory aspect of pain
    d. all of the above

6. The perception of pain may be influenced by (ref. pp. 301–304)

    a. context
    b. socialization
    c. attention
    d. all of the above

7. Athletes who continue to play despite being injured may be experiencing a short-term reduction of pain sensitivity due to. (ref. p. 301)

    a. sympathetic arousal
    b. parasympathetic arousal
    c. effective training and coaching
    d. activities that focus their attention on the pain

8. The McGill Pain Questionnaire yields a (ref. p. 302)

    a. pain threshold score
    b. pain rating and a pain intensity score
    c. pain tolerance and a pain intensity score
    d. pain rating and an encouraged tolerance level

9. Pain behaviors (ref. p. 302–304)

    a. are observable, measurable behaviors that are manifestations of chronic pain
    b. have proven useful in identifying the dynamics of different pain syndromes
    c. are utilized in assessing the impact of pain on quality of life
    d. all of the above

10. The sensory aspect of pain seems to be determined primarily by (ref. p. 305)

    a. A-delta fibers
    b. C-fibers
    c. the limbic system
    d. the cerebral cortex

11. The affective and motivational aspect of pain seems to be determined primarily by (ref. p. 305)

    a. A-delta fibers
    b. C-fibers
    c. endorphins
    d. the cerebral cortex

12. According to the gate theory, the experience of pain is (ref. p. 307)
   a. directly correlated with the amount of physical injury
   b. only slightly affected by psychological factors
   c. modified by cognitive, motivational, and emotional factors
   d. affected by psychological, but not social, factors

13. According to the gate theory, pain is experienced when (ref. pp. 307–308)
   a. the patterning of sensory stimulation exceeds a certain threshold
   b. the brain interprets the event as painful
   c. the spinal gate is opened
   d. all of the above

14. The influence of psychological processes is most clearly evident in the role that the gate control theory assigns to the (ref. pp. 307–308)
   a. central control mechanism
   b. gate mechanism in the dorsal horns of the spinal column
   c. peripheral nerve endings
   d. spinal column

15. Transmission (T) cells (ref. p. 308)
   a. modulate sensory stimulation from the periphery
   b. may have an excitatory or inhibitory influence on pain sensations to the brain
   c. inhibit the transmission of pain sensations through the brain stem
   d. none of the above

16. The gate control theory (ref. pp. 308)
   a. fails to account for the importance of sensory patterning in the experience of pain
   b. explains the role of psychological processes in pain but fails to explain the experience of different types of pain
   c. allows for a degree of specificity in the transmission of pain but minimizes the importance of overall patterning in the experience of pain
   d. integrates the importance of the sensory, affective, and evaluative components of pain

17. Endorphins are (ref. p. 308)
   a. substances produced by the substantia gelatinosa that help regulate pain
   b. substances produced by the brain and glands that help regulate pain
   c. specialized receptor sites that play an active role in the regulation of pain
   d. drugs, such as heroin and morphine, that help control pain

18. Endorphins appear to play a role in the (ref. p. 309)
   a. inhibition of pain
   b. stress response
   c. functioning of the immune system
   d. all of the above

19. Evaluations of efforts to employ opioids as long-term therapy for chronic pain indicate that opioid drugs may be successful in relieving (ref. p. 309)

 a. non-cancer pain

 b. cancer pain

 c. most chronic pain

 d. none of the above

20. Acute pain (ref. p. 309)

 a. is usually associated with anxiety and depression

 b. may precede the development of a chronic pain syndrome

 c. seldom responds to the administration of painkillers or other medication

 d. increases with the passage of time

21. Chronic low back pain and myofascial pain syndrome are examples of (ref. p. 310)

 a. acute pain

 b. chronic benign pain

 c. recurrent acute pain

 d. chronic progressive pain

22. Pain that persists longer than 6 months and increases in severity over time is considered to be (ref. p. 310)

 a. acute pain

 b. chronic benign pain

 c. recurrent acute pain

 d. chronic progressive pain

23. In comparison with acute pain patients, chronic pain patients (ref. p. 310)

 a. share a similar psychological profile

 b. experience higher levels of pain

 c. are more responsive to pain management techniques

 d. suffer from a syndrome involving physiological, psychological, social and behavioral components

24. According to Turk, Kerns, & Rosenberg (1992), chronic pain patients whose spouses provide support and positive attention (ref. p. 311)

 a. experience good marital and sexual functioning

 b. may inadvertently maintain or increase the expression of pain

 c. restrict their social contact to members of their immediate family

 d. take smaller amounts of pain killers than patients who do not receive such support

25. According to research investigating personality variables observed in chronic pain patients, (ref. p. 312)

 a. there is a pain-prone personality, which, like the disease-prone personality, is characterized by negative affectivity

 b. a significant proportion of the population appears to be predisposed to experience pain

 c. personality change is frequently a consequence of pain, but personality variables are seldom involved as causes

 d. different personality factors may be involved in different types of pain

26. Chronic pain patients typically show elevated scores on the following three MMPI subscales: (ref. p. 313)

    a. hysteria, hypochondriasis, and depression

    b. hypochondriasis, hysteria, and mania

    c. negative affectivity, hypochondriasis, and anxiety

    d. hypochondriasis, anxiety, and depression

27. Antidepressants combat pain by (ref. p. 314)

    a. reducing anxiety

    b. improving mood

    c. affecting neurotransmitters

    d. all of the above

28. The use of surgical techniques to control pain (ref. p. 315)

    a. involves the use of spinal blocks that block the upward transmission of impulses in the spinal column

    b. is becoming increasingly common as a treatment of last resort

    c. may result in only temporary improvement and have no lasting negative side effects

    d. may damage the nervous system and actually exacerbate chronic pain

29. Counterirritation relieves pain by (ref. p. 315)

    a. influencing the central control mechanism

    b. activating large fibers that close the spinal gate

    c. creating lesions in pain fibers and receptors

    d. influencing the transmission of pain impulses from the peripheral receptors

30. Biofeedback has been found to be (ref. p. 316)

    a. more effective in the reduction of muscle-tension headaches than relaxation training

    b. useful in the treatment of migraine but not muscle-tension headaches

    c. effective in providing long-term relief from the symptoms of Raynaud's disease

    d. successful through the conscious control of target physiological processes

31. Relaxation training strategies are (ref. p. 318)

    a. seldom effective by themselves and need to be combined with other methods of pain control

    b. generally less effective in reducing chronic pain than are meditation techniques

    c. effective in alleviating chronic but not acute pain

    d. all of the above

32. Controlled breathing is a component of (ref. p. 318)

    a. hypnosis

    b. relaxation training

    c. distraction

    d. acupuncture

33. Hypnosis relies on (ref. p. 318)
    a. physiological relaxation
    b. distraction
    c. reinterpretation of sensations
    d. all of the above

34. Acupuncture may (ref. p.319)
    a. function as a sensory method of controlling pain
    b. be effective because patients believe it will work
    c. trigger the release of endorphins
    d. all of the above

35. In general, distraction is most effective in reducing pain when (ref. p. 320)
    a. the pain is of high intensity
    b. the patient's attention is drawn to alternative tasks
    c. the pain is chronic
    d. suggestion or sensory redefinition is impractical

36. A study of the control of acute dental pain (Anderson, Baron, & Logan, 1991) found that distracting music (ref. p. 321)
    a. reported less distress than controls
    b. reduced stress but had no effect on pain
    c. reduced stress only if the music was coupled with a suggestion that it would effectively reduce stress
    d. none of the above

37. The results of a study of the use of coping techniques in pain management (Holmes & Stevenson, 1990) suggested that (ref. p. 321)
    a. avoidant coping was more effective in managing chronic pain
    b. attentional coping strategies were more effective in managing acute pain
    c. patients should be trained in avoidant or attentive coping strategies depending on the nature of their pain
    d. none of the above

38. In contrast to aggressive imagery, guided imagery (ref. p. 321)
    a. is more frequently used to combat pain
    b. induces a positive mood state
    c. focuses attention
    d. all of the above

39. Cognitive-behavioral pain interventions (ref. p. 322)
    a. encourage patients to entrust the management of their pain to the treatment team
    b. attempt to modify maladaptive cognitions but not overt and covert behaviors
    c. encourage clients to attribute their success to the treatment intervention
    d. none of the above

40. Of the cognitive-behavioral treatment strategies for pain management, those designed to target _____ may be especially helpful. (ref. p. 323)

    a. depression

    b. hostility

    c. hypochondriasis

    <u>d.</u> self-efficacy

41. Perceptions of self-efficacy have important implications in the management of chronic pain in that self-efficacy is associated with (ref. p. 323)

    a. lower levels of depression

    b. better adherence to treatment regimen

    c. physiological benefits such as opioid activation

    <u>d.</u> all of the above

42. Screening applicants for pain programs may be especially important in light of the fact that treatment efficacy has been found to be subject to individual differences in (ref. pp. 323–325)

    a. personality variables

    b. coping styles

    c. types of pain

    <u>d.</u> all of the above

43. Pain management programs incorporate (ref. pp. 323–325)

    a. the use of multiple techniques

    b. an interdisciplinary team of practitioners

    c. an evaluation of the patient's physical, emotional, and mental functioning

    <u>d.</u> all of the above

44. The incidence of relapse following initial successful treatment of persistent pain appears to range from about _____ to _____. (ref. p. 325)

    a. 10%; 90%

    <u>b.</u> 30%; 60%

    c. 50%; 75%;

    d. 60%; 90%

45. Relapse following initial successful treatment of pain is directly related to (ref. p. 325)

    a. lack of social support

    b. coping styles

    <u>c.</u> nonadherence to treatment regimen

    d. all of the above

Essay Questions

1. Explain how social psychological variables influence the perception of pain. (ref. pp. 301–302)

2. Use the gate theory of pain to explain why one sensation will be perceived as painful whereas another stimulus might not. (ref. pp. 307–308)

3. Pain control by use of physical or chemical techniques has long been used by health care providers. For which type of pain are they most useful, and why? (ref. pp. 314–315)

4. How effective are biofeedback, acupuncture, and hypnosis in pain management? Do they work better with some types of pain? Are they superior to simple distraction and relaxation? (ref. p. 316–321)

5. Describe the design and implementation of pain management programs. (ref. pp. 323–325)

CHAPTER 11
MANAGEMENT OF CHRONIC ILLNESS

Chapter Outline

I. Quality of Life

II. Emotional Responses to Chronic Illness

    A. Denial

    B. Anxiety

    C. Depression

    D. Are There Stages of Emotional Adjustment?

III. Coping with Chronic Disease

    A. Coping Strategies and Chronic Illness

    B. Patients' Beliefs About Chronic Illness

        1. Beliefs About the Nature of the Illness

        2. Beliefs About the Cause of the Illness

    C. Beliefs About the Controllability of the Illness

IV. Rehabilitation and Chronic Illness

    A. Physical Problems Associated with Chronic Illness

    B. Vocational Issues in Chronic Illness

    C. Social Interaction Problems in Chronic Illness

    D. Personal Issues in Chronic Illness

        1. The Physical Self

        2. The Achieving Self

        3. The Social Self

        4. The Private Self

    E. When the Chronically Ill Patient Is a Child

V. Interventions for Psychological Issues After Chronic Illness

A.   Pharmacological Interventions

B.   Individual Therapy

C.   Brief Psychotherapeutic Interventions

D.   Relaxation and Exercise

E.   Social Support Interventions

F.   Support Groups

Learning Objectives

1. Describe the prevalence of chronic illness in the United States.

2. Describe how quality of life is assessed.

3. Describe the emotional responses to chronic illness.

4. Explain the role of denial, anxiety, and depression in coping with chronic illness, and explain whether these emotional reactions occur in stages.

5. Explain the relationship of coping strategies to chronic illness.

6. Explain the role of patients' beliefs about the nature, cause, and controllability of their illness in their adjustment to chronic illness.

7. Describe the physical problems associated with chronic illness. Explain the nature and extent of nonadherence to rehabilitation regimens.

8. Describe the vocational issues associated with chronic illness.

9. Describe the social interaction problems associated with chronic illness.

10. Describe the personal issues associated with chronic illness.

11. Explain the psychological issues affecting the different aspects of the self (i.e., physical, achieving, social, and private self) associated with chronic illness.

12. Describe the unique issues faced by children coping with chronic illness.

13. Describe the use and effectiveness of pharmacological interventions in helping patients coping with chronic illness.

14. Describe the use and effectiveness of individual therapy in helping patients coping with chronic illness.

15. Describe the use and effectiveness of brief psychotherapeutic interventions in helping patients coping with chronic illness.

16. Describe the use and effectiveness of relaxation and exercise in helping patients coping with chronic illness.

17. Describe the use and effectiveness of social support interventions in helping patients coping with chronic illness.

18. Describe the use and effectiveness of support groups in helping patients coping with chronic illness.

Lecture Suggestions

The Negative Aspects of Personal Control

As noted in the text, there are instances when perceptions of control may not have a positive effect on adjustment to illness. The situations under which perceptions of control may have a negative impact on patients and their families are addressed in recent work by Thompson (1981; Thompson, Cheek, & Graham, 1988), which can be used to elaborate on the importance of control within this context.

Thompson, S. C. (1981). Will it hurt less if I can control it? A complex answer to a complex question. Psychological Bulletin, 90, 89–101.

Thompson, S. C., Cheek, P. R., & Graham, M. A. (1988). The other side of perceived control: Disadvantages and negative effects. In S. Spacapan and S. Oskamp (Eds.), The social psychology of health (pp. 69–93). Newbury Park: Sage.

Parental Coping with Chronically Ill Children

A series of studies by Affleck and his colleagues (Affleck, Allen, Tennen, McGrade, & Ratzan, 1985; Affleck, Tennen, & Gershman, 1985; Tennen, Affleck, & Gershman, 1986) have studied coping strategies of parents of high-risk infants and chronically ill children. The results of these studies are discussed in light of important themes of this text (e. g., mastery and control). Developing a lecture around these studies allows for a review of these concepts from the perspective of parents and other family members while addressing the special circumstances of the ill child.

Affleck, G., Allen, D. A., Tennen, H., McGrade, B. J., & Ratzan, S. (1985). Causal and control cognitions in parents' coping with chronically ill children. Journal of Social and Clinical Psychology, 3, 367–377.

Affleck, G., Tennen, H., & Gershman, K. (1985). Cognitive adaptations to high-risk infants: The search for mastery, meaning and protection from future harm. American Journal of Mental Deficiency, 87, 653–656.

Tennen, H., Affleck, G., & Gershman, K. (1986). Self-blame among parents of infants with perinatal complications: The role of self-protective motives. Journal of Personality and Social Psychology, 50, 690–696.

Case Studies

A number of vivid case studies may be found in a volume edited by McDaniel, Jepworth, and Doherty (1997) that reports case studies of therapeutic interventions with chronically ill patients and their families. The book is organized chronologically (childhood through old age), so examples from a number of age groups are easily available.

McDaniel, S. H., Jepworth, J., Doherty, W. J. (Eds.) (1997). <u>The shared experience of illness: Stories of patients, families, and their therapists</u>. New York: Basic Books.

Exercises, Projects, and Activities

The Impact of Chronic Illness

It is often useful to have students consider how their lives might be affected if they developed a chronic illness. This also provides an opportunity to discuss the very high probability that students will develop one or more chronic illnesses over their lifetimes. In addition, it allows a discussion of the wide range of chronic disorders (emphysema, asthma, hearing loss, etc.) that millions successfully manage on a daily basis. I have often found that many students write about chronic conditions that they now are struggling to manage. Some guidelines are presented below.

For this assignment you need to select one of the chronic illnesses discussed in class or in your text, and consider the ways in which your life might change if you had to cope with this condition on a daily basis. Then I would like you to consider your physical environment, your daily activities, your relationships with other people, and so on, and write an essay that addresses the following points.

1. Which chronic illness or disorder did you select? What symptoms are characteristic of this condition? What is the prognosis? What particular aspects of this illness may be particularly problematic in managing the day-to-day aspects of your illness?

2. Would any aspects of your physical environment have to be modified? Which ones? Why?

3. Would you need to change or modify any of your daily activities due to the demands of this condition? Which ones? Why?

4. Would you expect any of your relationships (from casual acquaintances to intimates) to change? Why? Do you feel that you might need a particular type of social support? Why?

5. Do you feel that your social network could provide you with effective social support? Why or why not? Do you feel that your support network would be strained because of your condition? Why or why not?

Support Groups

Invite a representative from a social support group (such as a Reach to Recovery volunteer) to speak to the class about the group's functions, members, and so on. A listing of organizations is usually available from local hospitals and county and state agencies.

Recommended Reading

Corbin, J. M., & Strauss, A. (1988). <u>Unending work and care: Managing chronic illness at home</u>. San Francisco: Jossey-Bass.

This book presents the impact of chronic illness on the patient, family, and friends. The management of different phases of chronic illness is discussed with an emphasis on the reciprocal relationship between clinical management of illness and family dynamics.

Thompson, R. J., & Gustafson, K. E. (1996). <u>Adaptation to chronic childhood illness</u>. Washington, DC: American Psychological Association.

This text, written for advanced students and professionals, takes a biopsychosocial approach to adjustment in pediatric samples. It provides a review of chronic illness within a developmental context, and outlines treatment goals, problems in adherence, and pain management.

Thorne, S. E. (1993). Negotiating health care: The social context of chronic illness. Newbury Park, CA: Sage.

This book summarizes the findings of a qualitative study of the treatment of chronically ill patients within the health care system. Patients interviewed discuss disease onset, management, and coping efforts.

True-False Questions

1. <u>T</u>   F   At any one time, 25% of the population has some chronic condition that requires medical treatment. (ref. p. 328)

2. T   <u>F</u>   The Sickness Impact Profile (SIP) yields scores for six functions (bathing, dressing, toileting, mobility, continence, and feeding). (ref. p. 330)

3. T   <u>F</u>   There is evidence that depression may occur somewhat earlier in the adjustment process than denial or severe anxiety. (ref. p. 334)

4. <u>T</u>   F   Certain positive emotions, such as joy and optimism, serve a protective function in recovery from illness. (ref. p. 335)

5. <u>T</u>   F   In general, active coping strategies seem to be more consistently associated with good adjustment to chronic illness than avoidant strategies. (ref. p. 337)

6. T   <u>F</u>   Research evidence consistently supports the notion that self-blame is associated with poor adjustment to chronic illness. (ref. p. 338)

7. <u>T</u>   F   Rehabilitation interventions designed to improve physical activity and independence are likely to improve daily functioning and adjustment to chronic illness. (ref. p. 341)

8. T   <u>F</u>   Due to the chronic strain involved, the divorce rate among families with a chronic illness is higher than that for the general population. (ref. p. 349)

9. <u>T</u>   F   The self-concept is a stable set of beliefs about one's qualities and attributes. (ref. p. 351)

10. T   <u>F</u>   Whereas disease severity and the presence of debilitating symptoms affect quality of life, they are unrelated to body image. (ref. p. 352)

Multiple-Choice Questions

1. Which of the following is **not** a chronic illness? (ref. p. 328)
   a. cancer
   b. hearing loss
   c. diabetes
   <u>d</u>. hepatitis

2. Quality of life traditionally has been measured in terms of (ref. p. 329)
   a. psychological and economic factors
   b. subjective criteria
   <u>c</u>. morbidity and mortality
   d. longevity

3. Physicians' ratings of quality of life are (ref. p. 329)
   a. seldom based on objective criteria
   <u>b</u>. poorly correlated with patients' and relatives' assessments
   c. poorly correlated with patients' assessments but are moderately correlated with relatives' assessments
   d. moderately correlated with health psychologists' assessments

4. The notion that quality of life is a subjective experience assumes that (ref. p. 329)
   <u>a</u>. patients may provide the most valid assessment of quality of life
   b. psychosocial and economic factors must be considered instead of measures of physiological functioning
   c. reliable and valid measures will never be developed
   d. quality of life is independent of changes in chronic illness and its treatment

5. Assessment of quality of life considers (ref. p. 330)
   a. disease- or treatment-related symptomatology
   b. physical status and functioning
   c. psychological and social status
   <u>d</u>. multiple criteria that includes all of the above

6. Adjustment to chronic illness differs from adjustment to acute illness in that chronic illness (ref. p. 331)
   a. includes a temporary first phase during which all life activities are disrupted
   b. requires patients to make intermittent or permanent changes in their activities, but such long-term changes are seldom associated with a crisis phase
   <u>c</u>. requires patients to adopt the sick role and integrate this role into their lives psychologically
   d. none of the above

7. Denial (ref. p. 332)
   a. is a defense mechanism that allows the patient to avoid the immediate implications of an illness
   b. results from the number of issues surrounding an illness and its treatment
   c. is a common reaction to chronic illness
   <u>d</u>. all of the above

8. Denial may serve a protective function (ref. p. 332)
   a. before the patient seeks medical treatment
   b. in the acute phase of the illness
   c. when patients must play an active role in the treatment regimen
   d. during the rehabilitative phase of the illness

9. Denial is useful in helping patients (ref. p. 332)
   a. control their emotional reaction to illness
   b. monitor their physical condition
   c. seek treatment
   d. become active in their treatment regimen

10. Of the following situations, patient anxiety would be highest (ref. p. 333)
    a. after the physician had explained the diagnosis and treatment regimen
    b. after the patient has received a test result
    c. while the patient is awaiting a new and promising, but invasive, medical procedure
    d. while the patient is experiencing the side effects of a familiar medical procedure

11. High levels of anxiety have been found among patients who are (ref. p. 333)
    a. anticipating noxious therapies
    b. expecting substantial lifestyle changes to result from illness or treatment
    c. lacking information about their illness and treatment
    d. all of the above

12. Disease-related anxiety may _____ over time, while anxiety related to the consequences of the disease may _____ over time. (ref. p. 333)
    a. decrease; decrease
    b. increase; increase
    c. increase; decrease
    d. decrease; increase

13. Up to _____ of all medical inpatients with chronic disease suffer from severe depression. (ref. p. 333)
    a. 10%
    b. 25%
    c. 33%
    d. 50%

14. Unlike anxiety and denial, depression may (ref. p. 334)
    a. be a long-term reaction to chronic illness
    b. ebb and flow during the course of chronic illness
    c. be the first response to chronic illness
    d. be intermittent and unrelenting

15. Depression in chronically ill patients is (ref. p. 334)
    a. independent of illness severity
    b. most commonly found in the acute phase of illness
    c. easily and reliably assessed
    d. related to long-term rehabilitation and recovery

16. Which of the following is **not** a predictor of depression among chronically ill patients? (ref. p. 335)
    a. lack of social support
    b. chronic pain
    c. marital status
    d. becoming disability

17. The emotional reactions to chronic illness (ref. p. 335)
    a. occur in an ordered sequence, first anxiety and denial, then depression
    b. have a negative impact on long-term rehabilitation and recovery
    c. influence patients' motivational, but not physical, state
    d. may serve a beneficial function in recovery from illness

18. According to a study of cancer patients conducted by Dunkel-Schetter and her colleagues (1988), the most frequently cited stressor was (ref. p. 336)
    a. fear and uncertainty about the future
    b. limitations in physical abilities
    c. pain management
    d. altered physical appearance and lifestyle

19. Analyses of the effectiveness of coping strategies in managing the stress associated with chronic illness conclude that (ref. p. 337)
    a. the coping strategies used by chronically ill patients are significantly different from the strategies observed in healthy samples
    b. avoidant coping is associated with reduced psychological distress and better psychological adjustment
    c. confrontative coping is associated with better adjustment than the use of multiple coping strategies
    d. active coping is associated with better adjustment among patients who also have high levels of perceived control

20. Successful adjustment to chronic illness is associated with (ref. p. 338)
    a. having an appropriate or accurate illness schema about the nature of one's illness
    b. developing an acute model of one's disorder
    c. blaming others for one's illness and thus minimizing self-blame
    d. having a personal sense of control, even in medical situations in which little personal control is possible

21. Studies evaluating the relationship between attributions and adjustment to chronic illness have found better adjustment among patients who attribute their illness to (ref. p. 339)
    a. internal factors
    b. environmental factors
    c. another person
    d. none of the above

22. In general, high levels of perceived control facilitate adjustment **except** in cases where (ref. p. 339)

    a. patients are seriously debilitated, both physically and psychosocially
    b. patients must cope with long-term chronic illness
    c. patients must cope with acute disorders and treatment
    d. where actual control is low

23. According to a study of myocardial infarction (MI) patients conducted by Bar-On & Dreman (1987), long-term rehabilitation was most successful when spouses held _____ attributions for the heart attack and their mates held _____ attributions for the heart attack. (ref. p. 340)

    a. external; external
    b. internal; internal
    c. internal; external
    d. external; internal

24. Which of the following is <u>not</u> one of the goals of rehabilitation discussed in your text? (ref. p. 341)

    a. redefining oneself as being chronically ill
    b. adherence to one's treatment regimen
    c. the control of energy expenditure
    d. the ability to identify and respond to the onset of a medical crisis

25. Chemotherapy may be accompanied by (ref. p. 342)

    a. changes in taste and the development of taste aversions
    b. burning of the skin
    c. gastrointestinal problems
    d. weight gain

26. Stress management programs are increasingly incorporated into physical treatment regimens due to the debilitating effects of stress on (ref. p. 343)

    a. psychosocial adjustment
    b. chronic diseases
    c. coping strategies
    d. none of the above

27. Adherence to treatment regimens in chronically ill patients is (ref. p. 343)

    a. significantly higher than in patients being treated for acute disorders
    b. significantly lower than in patients being treated for acute disorders
    c. unaffected by the side effects of treatment
    d. especially problematic in complex and long-term treatment regimens

28. Nonadherence to treatment regimens due to negative side effects is highest in patients undergoing (ref. p. 343)

    a. hypertension management programs
    b. chemotherapy
    c. insulin regimens
    d. none of the above

29. Adherence to treatment of hypertension and diabetes has been linked to (ref. p. 344)
    a. self-efficacy beliefs
    b. expectations that one's health is under one's own control
    c. information about treatment regimen
    d. all of the above

30. John Grey works with cancer patients at County General Hospital. His particular specialty is in enabling the newly diagnosed cancer patient to understand the illness and its treatment and to negotiate the difficult emotional and social identity issues associated with the illness. John is a (ref. pp. 346–347)
    a. medical social worker
    b. medical psychologist
    c. health psychologist
    d. occupational therapist

31. People may react particularly negatively to patients who are perceived to be (ref. p. 347)
    a. members of certain stigmatized groups, such as people with AIDS
    b. responsible for bringing on their condition
    c. failing to cope with their condition
    d. all of the above

32. Studies of reactions to the disabled indicate that they tend to elicit (ref. p. 347)
    a. pity
    b. curiosity
    c. ambivalence
    d. revulsion

33. Negative reactions to chronically ill patients include (ref. pp. 345–347)
    a. blatant discrimination
    b. nonverbal behavior communicating revulsion
    c. ambivalence
    d. all of the above

34. Adverse changes in social interactions after a diagnosis of chronic disease are more likely to be observed in (ref. p. 348)
    a. family members
    b. friends and acquaintances
    c. employers
    d. intimate others

35. Which of the following is **not** one of the factors associated with reducing the amount of social support provided by friends and family members to chronically ill patients? (ref. p. 348)
    a. pain, disability, and dependency of the patient
    b. unmet social support needs of the providers
    c. impaired communication with the patient
    d. none of the above

36. The importance of taking a systems approach to the management of social-interaction problems in chronic illness is demonstrated by the fact that (ref. p. 348)

   a. family members often neglect the chronically ill family member due to feelings of fear and aversion

   b. intimates may have trouble offering sufficient social support to the patient if their own support needs are unmet

   c. patients learn to improve their social skills by interacting with friends and acquaintances and generalize these new skills to family members

   d. all of the above

37. Researchers investigating gender differences in the receipt of social support have found that (ref. p. 349)

   a. disabled women are more effective than disabled men in establishing effective social support networks

   b. being married appears to protect men, but not women, from institutionalization

   c. married women spend fewer days in nursing homes than married men

   d. disabled men are less likely to be married than disabled women

38. The perception and evaluation of one's physical functioning and appearance comprises one's (ref. p. 352).

   a. physical self

   b. self-concept

   c. body image

   d. self-evaluation

39. Chronic alterations in one's body image would be most likely in cases of (ref. p. 352)

   a. chronic illness

   b. amputation

   c. extensive scarring

   d. facial disfigurement

40. The degree of threat to one's body image is influenced by (ref. p. 352)

   a. one's previous body image

   b. the amount of damage or scarring

   c. one's activity level

   d. all of the above

41. Because chronically ill children often cannot follow their treatment regimen by themselves (ref. p. 353)

   a. problematic parent-child interactions may result

   b. training the family in the treatment regimen can improve functioning

   c. interventions directed at either parents or children to the exclusion of the other may not be effective

   d. all of the above

42. Emotional disorders associated with chronic illness are especially likely among patients who (ref. p. 355)

   a. enter into very aggressive medical treatment regimens

   b. are motivated to find meaning and to compensate for any negative impact of chronic illness on their quality of life

   c. have a history of depression or other mental illness

   d. all of the above

43. Compared to therapy with other clients, psychotherapy provided to medical patients is more likely to (ref. p. 355)

   a. be continuous and long term in nature

   b. involve collaboration with the patient's family and physician

   c. be expensive and time consuming

   d. challenge the client's defenses and promote a realistic assessment of his or her situation

44. Coping-skills instruction appears to be successful due to (ref. p. 356)

   a. enhanced perceptions of control

   b. the provision of information about chronic disorders and their treatment

   c. improved interactions with others and enhanced social support

   d. all of the above

45. A social support group is most likely to appeal to (ref. p. 359)

   a. Fred, an insurance company executive who is recovering from a myocardial infarction (MI)

   b. María, a recent immigrant from the Philippines who suffers from rheumatoid arthritis

   c. Sybil, a high-school dropout with three children who is recovering from a mastectomy

   d. Edith, a physician who is also an ostomy patient

Essay Questions

1. Denial was once thought to be a primitive defense mechanism. What role does denial play in the emotional response to chronic illness? When does it facilitate coping? When is it dysfunctional? (ref. pp. 331–333)

2. How are patients' beliefs about chronic illness related to adjustment? (ref. pp. 337–340)

3. Explain why an interdisciplinary team approach to physical rehabilitation is superior to traditional programs. In your answer, cite material in the text about the problems of relapse and adherence to treatment regimens. (ref. pp. 340–340)

4. Studies have found that the quality of life reported by cancer patients is higher than healthy community samples. Explain how chronically ill patients cope with their illnesses and maintain a positive self-concept. (ref. pp. 350–353)

5. Explain the role of social support in coping with chronic illness. In your answer, consider both the benefits and the costs of social support. (ref. pp. 346–349; 357–358)

Chapter Outline

I.   Death Across the Life Span

    A.   Death in Infancy and Childhood

    B.   Death in Young Adulthood

    C.   Death in Middle Age

    D.   Death in Old Age

II.   Psychological Issues in Advancing Illness

    A.   Continued Treatment and Advancing Illness

    B.   Changes in the Patient's Self-Concept

    C.   Issues of Social Interaction

    D.   Communication Issues

    E.   The Issue of Nontraditional Treatment

III.   Are There Stages in Adjustment to Dying?

    A.   Kübler-Ross's Five-Stage Theory

        1.   Denial

        2.   Anger

        3.   Bargaining

        4.   Depression

        5.   Acceptance

    B.   Evaluation of Kübler-Ross's Theory

IV.   Psychological Management of the Terminally Ill

    A.   Medical Staff and the Terminally Ill Patient

        1.   The Significance of Medical Staff to the Patient

B.   Individual Counseling with the Terminally Ill

C.   Family Therapy with the Terminally Ill

D.   The Management of Terminal Illness in Children

V.   Alternatives to Hospital Care for the Terminally Ill

    A.   Hospice Care

        1.   Evaluating Hospice Care

    B.   Home Care

VI.   Problems of Survivors

    A.   The Adult Survivor

    B.   The Child Survivor

    C.   Death Education

Learning Objectives

1. Summarize the trends in infant mortality in the United States and describe the main causes of death in infancy and early childhood.

2. Describe the main causes of death in adolescence and adulthood.

3. Describe the nature of gender differences in mortality.

4. Describe the psychological issues associated with continued treatment and advancing illness.

5. Describe the Patient Self-Determination Act and explain the issues associated with euthanasia and assisted suicide.

6. Describe the changes in patient's self-concept that are associated with advancing illness.

7. Explain the issues of social interaction, communication, and nontraditional treatment associated with advancing illness.

8. Explain Kübler-Ross's Five-Stage theory and evaluate its value as a model of death and dying.

9. Describe the significance of the medical staff to the terminally ill patient.

10. Describe the physician's role and the role of other medical staff in terminal care.

11. Describe the nature of individual counseling and family therapy with the terminally ill.

12. Describe the nature of the management of terminal illness in children.

13. Describe the nature of hospice care and home, and evaluate the effectiveness of each.

14. Describe the problems faced by the adult and child survivors.

15. Describe the nature of death education.

Lecture Suggestions

The Terminal Phase of Life

Schulz's (1978; Schulz & Schlarb, 1991) reviews of death and dying in American culture are good resources for the development of lecture material to supplement Chapter 12. Topics addressed in this volume include an analysis of the terminal phase of life, including the responses of staff and the needs of the patient. In addition, the author reviews the sociological and psychological literature relating to euthanasia, grief and bereavement, medical and legal definitions of death, and death education.

Schulz, R. (1978). The psychology of death, dying, and bereavement. Reading, MA: Addison-Wesley.

Schulz, R., & Schlarb, J. (1991). Two decades of research on dying: What do we know about the patient? In A. Monat, R. S. Lazarus (Eds.), Stress and coping: An anthology. New York: Columbia University Press.

Death and Burnout Among Health Care Practitioners and Families

The articles referenced below present an analysis of the burnout suffered by health care practitioners who work with terminally ill patients. This topic may supplement the text's presentation of survivors' reactions to death. It also presents interventions to facilitate coping with death-related burnout.

Marquis, S. (1993). Death of the nursed: Burnout of the provider. Omega: Journal of Death and Dying, 27, 17–33.

Perreault, Y. (1995). AIDS grief: "Out of the closet and into the boardrooms": The bereaved caregivers. Journal of Palliative Care, 11, 34–37.

Plante, A., & Bouchard, L. (1995). Occupational stress, burnout, and professional support in nurses working with dying patients. Omega: Journal of Death and Dying, 32, 93–109.

Expressing One's Grief and Bereavement

As mentioned in the text, George Bonanno and colleagues (Bonanno & Keltner, 1997; Bonanno, Keltner, Holen, & Horowitz, 1995; Horowitz & Bonanno, 1993) are making the often controversial assertion that expressing one's grief is not associated with positive adjustment to the loss of a loved one. This research might be discussed in light of Pennebaker's work on catharsis and coping (see Chapter 7) and the cross-cultural perspectives on grief and bereavement from this chapter.

Bonanno, G. A., & Keltner, D. (1997). Facial expressions of emotion and the course of conjugal bereavement. Journal of Abnormal Psychology, 106, 126–137.

Bonanno, G. A., Keltner, D., Holen, A., & Horowitz, M. J. (1995). When avoiding unpleasant emotions might not be such a bad thing: Verbal-autonomic response dissociation and midlife conjugal bereavement. Journal of Personality and Social Psychology, 69, 975–989.

Horowitz, M. J., Bonanno, G. A., & Holen, A. (1993). Pathological grief: Diagnosis and explanation. Psychosomatic Medicine, 55, 260–273.

Exercises, Projects, and Activities

Living Wills

As the text notes, a number of recent court decisions have made the issue of the extension of life by extraordinary measures a timely topic. Discussing the conditions under which the termination of medical treatment is appropriate should elicit active student participation. Although laws vary from state to state (and legislation currently is pending in many states), the text from a generic living will document that has been used in California is reproduced below. Students should be advised that this form may not be legally valid; it is for discussion purposes only. As the text notes, documents of this nature may take a number of forms. For example, many documents have the executor delete the measures he or she would not want medical personnel to undertake in the case of serious advancing illness. It should be noted that the language of this document is somewhat vague and may allow for a number of differing interpretations.

A LIVING WILL

TO MY FAMILY, MY PHYSICIAN, MY LAWYER, MY CLERGYMAN

TO ANY MEDICAL FACILITY IN WHOSE CARE I HAPPEN TO BE

TO ANY INDIVIDUAL WHO MAY BECOME RESPONSIBLE FOR MY HEALTH, WELFARE, OR AFFAIRS

Death is as much a reality as birth, growth, maturity and old age--it is the one certainty of life. If the time comes when I, _____, can no longer take part in decisions for my own future, let this statement stand as an expression of my wishes, while I am still of sound mind.

If the situation should arise in which there is no reasonable expectation of my recovery from physical or mental disability, I request that I be allowed to die and not be kept alive by artificial means or "heroic measures." I do not fear death itself as much as the indignities of deterioration, dependence, and hopeless pain. I, therefore, ask that medication be mercifully administered to me to alleviate suffering even though this may hasten the moment of death.

This request is made after careful consideration. I hope you who care for me will feel morally bound to follow its mandate. I recognize that this appears to place a heavy responsibility upon you, but it is with the intention of relieving you of such responsibility and of placing it upon myself in accordance with my strong convictions, that this statement is made.

Date_____ Signed_____

Witness_____ Witness_____

Witness_____ Witness_____

Copies of this request have been given to: _____

(Source: Euthanasia Educational Council, New York.)

Attitudes Toward Death

Personal and cultural attitudes toward death may be explored by administering the Dimensions of Death Anxiety Scale (Nelson & Nelson, 1975). This instrument measures four dimensions of death anxiety (death avoidance, fear of death, death denial, and reluctance to interact with the dying), which may be used to discuss the issues surrounding death and dying in American culture.

Nelson, L. D., & Nelson, C. C. (1975). A factor analytic inquiry into the multidimensionality of death anxiety. Omega: Journal of Death and Dying, 6, 171–178.

Recommended Reading

Brody, E. B. (1993). Biomedical technology and human rights. Aldershot: Dartmouth Publishing Company, Ltd.

This book, directed at a professional audience, discusses human rights and biomedical ethics in a number of cultural and medical contexts. Of particular interest is a chapter on the ethical issues of sustaining the life of dying or comatose patients.

Dickenson, D., & Johnson, M. (1993). Death, dying, and bereavement. London: Sage Publications.

This edited book, written for the advanced student and professionals, addresses topics such as pain control, guidelines for counseling the bereaved, attitudes toward euthanasia, etc. It also contains a number of anecdotes and interviews with patients, family members, and caregivers.

Kübler-Ross, E. (1969). On death and dying. New York: Macmillan.

This book originally presented Kübler-Ross's theory to the general audience. It provides a rich description of the personal and social processes associated with dying in this culture. It also contains a number of revealing interviews with patients, practitioners, and family members.

True-False Questions

1. T   F   As reproductive technology has improved over the past decade, the infant mortality rate for black infants has declined. (ref. p. 369)

2. T   F   The major cause of death in youths aged 15 to 24 is unintentional injury. (ref. p. 369)

3. T   <u>F</u>   Compared to 15 years ago, Americans aged 65 and older experience better quality of life and reduced mortality. (ref. p. 376)

4. T   <u>F</u>   The Patient Self-Determination Act requires that all health care facilities in the United States have written policies and procedures concerning patients wishes for life-prolonging therapy. (ref. p. 378)

5. <u>T</u>   F   One plausible scientific explanation for the success of some nontraditional   treatments is the placebo effect. (ref. p. 384)

6. <u>T</u>   F   Long-term denial of a terminal illness should be a target of therapeutic intervention. (ref. p. 384)

7. T   <u>F</u>   Kübler-Ross's theory has made an important contribution in identifying the universal stages of dying and breaking the taboo surrounding death. (ref. p. 386)

8. <u>T</u>   F   The development of a sense that one is leaving behind a legacy through one's children or one's work is termed "symbolic immortality." (ref. p. 389)

9. T   <u>F</u>   Hospice care involves accepting death in a positive manner and assisted suicide. (ref. p. 392)

10. T   <u>F</u>   Studies of patient satisfaction and medical outcomes have clearly established that hospice care is superior to traditional terminal care. (ref. p. 393)

Multiple-Choice Questions

1. The infant mortality rate in the United States (ref. p. 369)
   a. is higher than that in most Western European countries
   b. is twice as high for black infants as for white infants
   c. may be associated with inequities in access to health care
   <u>d</u>. all of the above

2. Poor adjustment for parents of children who have died from SIDS is associated with (ref. p. 369)
   a. maternal smoking
   <u>b</u>. self-blame
   c. socioeconomic status
   d. all of the above

3. After infancy, the main cause of death among children under age 15 is (ref. p. 369)
   a. acute illness
   b. SIDS
   <u>c</u>. accidents
   d. cancer, especially leukemia

4. The only cause of childhood death that has **not** declined over the last decade is (ref. p. 370)
   <u>a</u>. homicide
   b. SIDS
   c. accidents
   d. leukemia

5. Walt's parents have explained to him that his grandmother has died. He keeps asking them questions about her death, where she is, and when he can see her. Walt is most likely (ref. p. 370)

   a. 4 years old

   b. 6 years old

   c. 9 years old

   d. 12 years old

6. Children typically do not attain an adult understanding of death until (ref. p. 370)

   a. roughly the age of 5

   b. between the ages of 5-9

   c. between the ages of 9-10

   d. adolescence

7. Mainstreaming children with leukemia (ref. p. 371)

   a. involves a comprehensive program that includes the entire family and the child's home and school environment

   b. involves intensive family therapy that takes a systems approach

   c. is seldom an issue since the survival rate for childhood leukemia is very low

   d. is seldom successful since school-aged children react with profound fear and aversion to the leukemic child's appearance and the stigma of cancer

8. According to the text, one important contributing factor to mid-life crisis is the (ref. p. 372)

   a. gradual realization of impending death

   b. growing awareness that one's risk factors for chronic illness are increasing

   c. cultural emphasis placed on youth

   d. declining importance middle-aged adults place on their work

9. The main cause of premature death in adulthood is sudden death due to (ref. p. 372)

   a. accidents

   b. stroke or heart attack

   c. AIDS

   d. homicide

10. After the Surgeon General issued his health guidelines in 1979, the death rate among young adults aged 25 to 65 declined, due to a 60% drop in (ref. p. 372)

    a. stroke

    b. heart disease

    c. cancers

    d. all of the above

11. Death in the elderly is (ref. p. 373)

    a. more likely to be sudden

    b. less likely to be due to degenerative diseases

    c. usually accompanied by a shorter terminal phase

    d. usually protracted because there is often more than one biological competitor for death

12. Which of the following is **not** one of the factors that has been found to predict mortality in the elderly age group? (ref. p. 374)
    a. close family relationships
    b. depression
    c. reduced life satisfaction
    d. hardiness

13. Which of the following is **not** cited by your text as one of the factors that contribute to women's lower mortality rates? (ref. p. 375)
    a. biological fitness
    b. health beliefs
    c. fewer risky behaviors
    d. social support

14. The Patient Self-Determination Act (ref. p. 378)
    a. applies only to hospice patients
    b. requires Medicare and Medicaid facilities to have documented policies concerning patients' wishes for life-prolonging therapy
    c. has legalized passive euthanasia
    d. is opposed by most Americans

15. A living will outlines (ref. p. 380)
    a. a patient's wishes to undergo euthanasia
    b. a patient's request that extraordinary life-sustaining procedures not be used
    c. the conditions under which a patient requests to remain alive
    d. the disposition of one's belongings after death

16. Which of the following is **not** one of the problematic issues surrounding euthanasia and assisted suicide cited in your text? (ref. p. 382)
    a. Increasingly negative attitudes in the general public to euthanasia and assisted suicide
    b. Inequity of access to life-sustaining medical technologies
    c. Lack of guidelines regarding cost-effectiveness and appropriateness of use
    d. Lack of consensus on the appropriate roles of the individual and health care practitioners

17. Emotional and social withdrawal in terminally ill patients is (ref. p. 382)
    a. successfully treated with antidepressants
    b. always due to anticipatory grieving
    c. an expected and common occurrence
    d. all of the above

18. As a patient's prognosis worsens, interpersonal communications often deteriorate. The reasons for this breakdown are generally due to (ref. p. 383)
    a. ambivalence and conflict
    b. long-term communication problems in the family
    c. indifference among medical staff members
    d. fear and aversion

19. Patients are **less** likely to turn to alternative treatments when they are satisfied (ref. p. 384)

a. with the interpersonal aspects of their medical care

b. with the technical aspects of their medical care

c. that the costs of medical care can be borne by their families

d. that there is still something more the medical establishment can do for their condition

20. The correct order of Kübler-Ross's stages of adjustment to dying are (ref. p. 384)

a. depression, anger, bargaining, denial, acceptance

b. denial, anger, bargaining, acceptance, depression

c. denial, bargaining, anger, depression, acceptance

d. denial, anger, bargaining, depression, acceptance

21. Lazarus (1983) argues that _____ serves a protective function in adjustment to advancing illness. (ref. p. 384)

a. anxiety

b. bargaining

c. denial

d. anger

22. Long-term denial of impending death (ref. p. 384)

a. is a typical reaction

b. is functional in coping with anxiety

c. may require psychological intervention

d. none of the above

23. According to Kübler-Ross, the dying patient who asks "why me?" is experiencing (ref. p. 385)

a. anxiety

b. bargaining

c. denial

d. anger

24. According to Kübler-Ross, the dying patient who is coming to terms with his or her understanding that the world is just is most likely experiencing (ref. p. 385)

a. denial

b. depression

c. bargaining

d. acceptance

25. The depressed terminally ill patient may be (ref. p. 385)

a. coming to terms with a lack of control

b. experiencing anticipatory grief

c. experiencing an expected transitory psychological state, which may not require intervention

d. all of the above

26. Kübler-Ross's theory of death and dying (ref. p. 386)
    a. accurately identifies the stages of the dying process
    b. acknowledges the importance of death-related anxiety
    c. has broken the taboo surrounding death
    d. all of the above

27. According to a review by Schulz and Aderman (1974), the one consistency observed in studies of the process of dying is the common expression of _____ prior to death. (ref. p. 472)
    a. anger
    b. anxiety
    c. denial
    d. depression

28. According to critics, Kübler-Ross's theory fails to acknowledge the frequency with which dying patients experience (ref. p. 386)
    a. anxiety
    b. enhanced perceptions of control
    c. depression
    d. social support

29. According to Turk and Feldman (1992a, 1992b), the hospitalized terminally ill patient runs the risk of being (ref. p. 387)
    a. ignored by the medical staff
    b. isolated by the medical staff
    c. overmedicated by the medical staff
    d. undermedicated by the medical staff

30. Palliative care involves (ref. p. 387)
    a. final attempts to cure the terminally ill patient
    b. life-prolonging interventions such as placing the patient on a respirator
    c. ending the life of a patient who is suffering from a painful terminal illness
    d. custodial work designed to make the patient feel comfortable

31. Medical staff who are sensitive to the problem of communication problems when working with the terminally ill should ensure that information is provided to the patient in a manner that is (ref. p. 388)
    a. consistent and open
    b. detached but efficient
    c. emotionally expressive
    d. in accordance with the family's wishes

32. Cultural differences have been found in beliefs about whether patients (ref. p. 388)
    a. should be informed of all prognoses, terminal or not
    b. should make the decision about the use of life support
    c. work through stages of dying
    d. all of the above

33. Which of the following is **not** one of the goals of medical staff who work with the dying? (ref. p. 389)

    a. Informing patients of their prognosis and treatment

    <u>b</u>. Helping patients live as long as possible

    c. Enabling patients and their families to experience anticipatory grief.

    d. Involving patients in their treatment, as appropriate.

34. Making a terminally ill patient an informed participant in medical care decisions may be useful in (ref. p. 389)

    a. enhancing feelings of personal control

    b. providing a sense of predictability about one's medical condition and its treatment

    c. allaying helplessness and depression

    <u>d</u>. all of the above

35. Therapy with the dying differs from traditional psychotherapy in that it is likely to be (ref. p. 389)

    a. episodic

    b. initiated by the patient

    c. similar to therapy with the chronically ill

    <u>d</u>. none of the above

36. Research suggests that cognitive-behavioral therapy can be employed with dying patients (Sobel, 1981), especially (ref. p. 389)

    <u>a</u>. positive self-talk

    b. self-monitoring

    c. systematic desensitization

    d. all of the above

37. Terminally ill children (ref. p. 390)

    a. are unable to understand most information relevant to their medical condition and treatment

    <u>b</u>. use cues from their treatment and others' responses to infer the nature of their medical condition

    c. generally believe that they will soon recover and go home

    d. do not hesitate to express their concerns and questions directly to others

38. For which of the following patients would hospice care be most appropriate? (ref. p. 391)

    a. John, aged 75, who suffers from chronic emphysema

    b. Joe, aged 50, who suffered a paralyzing stroke

    <u>c</u>. John, aged 20, who has terminal cancer

    d. Frieda, aged 90, who is suffering from heart disease

39. The goals of hospice care include (ref. p. 392)

    a. palliative care

    b. psychological comfort

    c. improved social support

    <u>d</u>. all of the above

40. Hospices (ref. p. 393)
   a. have had only limited success as a treatment model
   b. are seldom affiliated with hospitals due to fears of malpractice litigation
   c. are increasingly incorporated into traditional treatment
   d. are providing more individualized care than in the past

41. Evaluations of hospice care indicate that, compared to patients who receive traditional treatment, hospice patients (ref. p. 393)
   a. live longer
   b. receive fewer invasive procedures
   c. report lower levels of anxiety
   d. are more satisfied with their interpersonal care

42. According to the research cited in your text, the majority of terminally ill patients and their families prefer (ref. pp. 393–395)
   a. home care
   b. hospice care
   c. traditional hospital care
   d. skilled nursing facilities

43. Competent home care for the terminally ill requires (ref. p. 394)
   a. adequate training of family members
   b. regular contact between medical personnel and family members
   c. a division of around-the-clock responsibilities between family members
   d. all of the above

44. Compared to other cultures, death in America (ref. pp. 394–395)
   a. is surrounded by taboo
   b. occurs in the absence of family members
   c. is accompanied by social pressures against the expression of emotion
   d. all of the above

45. The grief response appears to be aggravated in (ref. p. 397)
   a. women and those who experience sudden and unexpected loss
   b. men and those who experience sudden and unexpected loss
   c. survivors whose family members have experienced a protracted and painful death
   d. young children who experience the death of a sibling

Essay Questions

1. Explain the medical, social, and psychological factors associated with continuing treatment of a terminal illness. What options are now available to terminally ill patients and their families? (ref. pp. 377–384)

2. Describe Kübler-Ross's theory of dying. Evaluate the usefulness of her theory. (ref. pp. 384–387).

3. Suppose you were working in a facility that provided care for terminally ill patients and their families. What psychosocial factors would be important for you to consider in training staff members? Why? (ref. pp. 387–391).

4. There has been a great deal of interest in hospice and home care for the terminally ill. What are the advantages of each for patients and careproviders (both family and medical staff)? What are the disadvantages? (ref. pp. 391–395)

5. Describe the psychological and physiological correlates of grief. (ref. pp. 395–397)

CHAPTER 13
HEART DISEASE, HYPERTENSION, STROKE, AND DIABETES

Chapter Outline

I. Coronary Heart Disease

    A.   Type A Behavior

    B.   Cardiovascular Reactivity, Hostility, and CHD

    C.   Mechanisms Linking Reactivity and Hostility to CHD

    D.   Negative Emotions, Risk Factors, and CHD

    E.   Modification of CHD Risk-Related Behavior

II. Management of Myocardial Infarction

    A.   Cardiac Rehabilitation

    B.   Problems of Social Support

    C.   Psychosocial Responses to MI

III. Hypertension

    A.   Overview

    B.   Relationship Between Stress and Hypertension

    C.   Personality Factors and Hypertension

    D.   Treatment of Hypertension

        1.   Overview

        2.   Drug Treatments

        3.   Cognitive-Behavioral Treatments

    E.   Problems in Treating Hypertension

IV. Stroke

    A.   Consequences of Stroke

    B.   Types of Rehabilitative Interventions

V. Management of Diabetes

A.   Types of Diabetes

B.   Implications of Diabetes

C.   Causes of Diabetes

D.   Problems in Self-Management of Diabetes

E.   Interventions with Diabetics

F.   Special Problems of Adolescent Diabetics

Learning Objectives

1.   Describe the prevalence of CHD in the United States.

2.   Describe the nature of CHD and outline the risk factors that are implicated in its development.

3.   Discuss the nature of gender differences in medical research and risk factors for CHD.

4.   Describe the Type A behavior pattern and summarize research investigating the relationship between Type A behavior and CHD.

5.   Describe the relationship of cardiovascular reactivity, hostility, and CHD.

6.   Summarize the research investigating the relationship between negative emotions and CHD.

7.   Describe the techniques used to modify CHD risk-related behavior and evaluate their effectiveness.

8.   Describe the nature and prevalence of myocardial infarction in the United States.

9.   Explain the process of cardiac rehabilitation and the typical MI treatment regimens.

10. Describe the issues surrounding the implementation of lifestyle changes following MI.

11. Describe the problems with social support following MI.

12. Describe the psychosocial responses to MI.

13. Describe the nature and prevalence of hypertension in the United States.

14. Explain the relationship between stress and hypertension.

15. Summarize the results of research investigating the relationship between personality factors and hypertension.

16. Define John Henryism and explain how this phenomenon may explain hypertension risk in low-SES black Americans.

17. Describe treatment regimens prescribed for hypertension, including drug and cognitive-behavioral treatments.

18. Discuss the problems in treating hypertension.

19. Describe the nature and prevalence of stroke in the United States.

20. Describe the physical, psychological, social, and emotional consequences of stroke.

21. Describe the types of rehabilitative interventions for stroke.

22. Describe the nature and prevalence of diabetes in the United States.

23. Compare and contrast Type I and Type II diabetes.

24. Describe the implications of diabetes, especially the problems of hypoglycemia and hyperglycemia.

25. Explain the causes of diabetes.

26. Describe the problems in self-management of diabetes. Discuss the problems in adherence to treatment regimens and the factors that predict adherence.

27. Describe behaviorally oriented interventions with diabetics and evaluate their effectiveness.

28. Discuss the special problems faced by adolescent diabetics.

Lecture Suggestions

Secondary Prevention in Respiratory Disorders

The prevention and management of another chronic disorder, asthma, may be introduced as a supplementary lecture topic. Defares and Grossman's (1988) chapter is a useful source of lecture material for a discussion of the role of stress in respiratory disorders, and Kaptein, Dekker, Van der Waart, and Gill (1988) provide a review of the research on asthma. Two sources for information about treatment options are Culpert and colleagues' (1996) work with teaching biofeedback to pediatric patients and Maes and Schlosser's (1988, 1989) cognitive-behavioral management program developed for asthmatics.

Culpert, T. P., Kajander, R. L., & Reaney, J. B. (1996). Biofeedback with children and adolescents: Clinical observations and patient perspectives. Journal of Developmental and Behavioral Pediatrics, 17, 342–350.

Defares, P. B., & Grossman, P. (1988). Hyperventilation, stress, and high-risk behavior. In S. Maes, C.D. Spielberger, P. B. Defares, & I. G. Sarason (Eds.), Topics in health psychology. Chichester: Wiley.

Kaptein, A. A., Dekker, F. W., Van der Waart, A. C., & Gill, K. (1988). Health psychology and asthma: Current status and future directions. In S. Maes, C. D. Spielberger, P. B. Defares, & I. G. Sarason (Eds.), Topics in health psychology. Chichester: Wiley.

Maes, S. & Schlosser, M. (1988). The cognitive management of health behavior outcomes in asthmatic patients. In S. Maes, C. D. Spielberger, P. B. Defares, & I. G. Sarason (Eds.), Topics in health psychology. Chichester: Wiley.

Maes, S., & Schlosser, M. (1989). The role of cognition and coping in health behavior outcomes of asthmatic patients. In M. Johnston and T. Marteau (Eds.), Applications in health psychology (pp. 109–120). New Brunswick: Transaction.

Ethnic Differences in Coronary Heart Disease

A special issue of Health Psychology (1989, Volume 8, No. 5) was dedicated to race, reactivity, and blood pressure regulation. This issue would provide a valuable source of lecture material for a discussion of ethnic and gender differences in coronary heart disease. Another, more recent issue (1995, Volume 14, No. 7) also addresses sociocultural and behavioral factors relevant to ethnicity and health.

Hypertension and Chronic Folk Illness

Heurtin-Roberts (1993) presents an interesting study of 60 older African-American women's beliefs about hypertension. She argues that this sample's beliefs reflected the use of a chronic folk illness, "high-pertension," or a chronic "nervous" condition related to the blood as a method of coping with their social environment. She asserts that chronic folk illnesses may reflect a strategy of expressing one's self within the social context. Thus, health beliefs about chronic illnesses may serve a role in adaptation and managing one's environment.

Heurtin-Roberts, S. (1993). "High-pertension": The uses of a chronic folk illness for personal adaptation. Social Science and Medicine, 37, 285–294.

Coping with Stroke

The topic of stroke may be developed for classroom lectures. Students often think that stroke is a disease of the elderly when, in fact, young adults are increasingly likely to become victims of this disorder. Krantz and Deckel (1983) present an overview of disabilities related to coronary heart disease and stroke. Gordon and Diller's (1983) chapter describes the management of the cognitive deficits related to stroke. They compare the effects of left- and right-hemispheric damage, and discuss the special problems of patients suffering from affective disorders.

Gordon, W. A., & Diller, L. (1983). Stroke: Coping with a cognitive deficit. In T. G. Burish & L. A. Bradley (Eds.), Coping with chronic disease: Research and applications. New York: Academic Press.

Krantz, D. S., & Deckel, A. W. (1983). Coping with coronary heart disease and stroke. In T. G. Burish & L. A. Bradley (Eds.), Coping with chronic disease: Research and applications. New York: Academic Press.

Stress and Diabetes

The role of stress in the management of diabetes may be a useful lecture topic. Bradley (1988) discusses the avenues by which stress can trigger diabetic symptoms as well as individual differences in reactivity to stress and stress management. Turk and Speers (1983) present the role of psychological appraisal in exacerbating diabetic decompensation. They also discuss problems of adherence and self-care regimens.

Bradley, C. (1988). Stress and diabetes. In S. Fisher & J. Reason (Eds.), Handbook of life stress, cognition, and health. Chichester: Wiley.

Turk, D. C., & Speers, M. A. (1983). Diabetes mellitus: A cognitive-functional analysis of stress. In T. G. Burish & L. A. Bradley (Eds.), Coping with chronic disease: Research and applications (pp. 147–169). New York: Academic Press.

Exercises, Projects, and Activities

Risk Profiles for Coronary Heart Disease

Have students work in small groups in order to identify their personal risk factors for coronary heart disease. This will provide an opportunity to review the risk factors described in the text within the context of their personal health habits.

The Type A Campus

Levine, Lynch, Miyake, and Lucia (1989) conducted an interesting field study of the pace of city life and its relationship to coronary heart disease. Students may use their indicators of pace (i.e., walking speed, articulation rate, work speed, and the proportion of individuals wearing watches) to evaluate the pace of life on campus. Classroom discussion might attend to the relationship of these variables to Type A behaviors as assessed by the Jenkins Activity Survey (Jenkins, Zyzanski, & Rosenman, 1971) and other measures.

Jenkins, C. D., Zyzanski, S. J., & Rosenman, R. H. (1971). Progress toward validation of a computer-scored test for the Type A coronary-prone behavior pattern. Psychosomatic Medicine, 33, 193–202.

Levine, R. V., Lynch, K., Miyake, K., & Lucia, M. (1989). The Type A city: Coronary heart disease and the pace of life. Journal of Behavioral Medicine, 12, 509–524.

Recommended Reading

Friedman, M., & Rosenman, R. H. (1974). Type A behavior and your heart. New York: Knopf.

The authors present an overview of the relationship of Type A behavior and coronary heart disease to a general audience.

Allan, R., & Scheidt, S. S. (Eds.) (1996). Heart and mind: The practice of cardiac psychology. Washington, DC: American Psychological Association.

This volume provides a comprehensive review of the medical and psychological literature relevant to coronary heart disease. Topics range from Type A behavior patterns, to prevention of CHD, and issues relevant to treatment and rehabilitation.

Siegman, A. W., & Smith, T. W. (1994). Anger, hostility, and the heart. Hillsdale: Erlbaum.

This edited volume summarizes research on the role of anger and hostility on the etiology and course of coronary heart disease. Chapters address such topics as the history of coronary-prone behavior, assessment issues, animal models of aggression and cardiovascular disease, etc.

True-False Questions

1. T   F   Diabetes is a risk factor for coronary heart disease. (ref. p. 401)

2. T   F   Across the life span, women seem to be protected against coronary heart disease relative to men. (ref. p. 402)

3. T   F   Whereas Type A behavior may be related to poor health, research has discounted its role in the development of coronary heart disease. (ref. p. 404)

4. T   F   Social support appears to be protective for women and men in terms of daily blood pressure increases in response to stress. (ref. p. 406)

5. T   F   Booth-Kewley and Friedman (1987) concluded that coronary proneness may be characterized more by negative emotional states than the Type A behavior pattern. (ref. p. 407)

6. T   F   Aspirin has been found to significantly reduce the risk for fatal heart attack, at least in men. (ref. p. 411)

7. T   F   Mild hypertension is defined by a diastolic pressure consistently between 105 and 119. (ref. p. 416)

8. <u>T</u>   F   Variations in blood pressure are especially high among smokers, heavy drinkers, and people under stress. (ref. p. 417)

9. <u>T</u>   F   The mortality rate is around 30% during the first month after a stroke. (ref. p. 424)

10. T   <u>F</u>   Whereas stress adversely affects adherence to treatment and diet, stress has not been found to directly affect Type I and Type II diabetes. (ref. p. 429)

Multiple-Choice Questions

1. The number one killer in the United States, accounting for 40% of all deaths, is (ref. p. 401)
    <u>a</u>. coronary heart disease
    b. hypertension
    c. diabetes
    d. cancer

2. Angina pectoris is (ref. p. 401)
    a. narrowing of the coronary arteries
    b. hardening of the coronary arteries
    <u>c</u>. pain resulting from a shortage of oxygen
    d. none of the above

3. Which of the following is <u>not</u> one of the risk factors for coronary heart disease? (ref. p. 401)
    a. hypertension
    b. high serum cholesterol
    c. cigarette smoking
    <u>d</u>. alcohol consumption

4. Which of the following job factors has been found to be related to increased risk of CHD? (ref. p. 401)
    a. high work pressure
    b. underemployment
    c. low job security
    <u>d</u>. all of the above

5. Women (ref. p. 402)
    a. show greater increases in cardiovascular neuorendocrine and some metabolic responses in response to stress than do men
    <u>b</u>. experience an increased risk of myocardial infarction or CHD-related death after menopause
    c. develop CHD on the average about 15 years earlier than do men
    d. seem to be protected at young ages against CHD due to their lower levels of HDL cholesterol

6. Which of the following would be **least** effective in preventing further damage and subsequent heart attacks in individuals diagnosed with coronary heart disease? (ref. p. 403)

    a. reducing serum cholesterol

    b. switching to low tar and nicotine cigarettes

    c. modifying behavioral methods of coping with stress

    d. reducing substantially elevated blood pressure

7. The Type A behavior pattern is characterized by (ref. p. 403)

    a. hostility, time urgency, and competitive achievement strivings

    b. negative affectivity, hostility, and competitive achievement strivings

    c. commitment, chronic stress, and time urgency

    d. commitment, hostility, and competitive achievement strivings

8. The structured interview designed to measure Type A behavior measures a subject's (ref. p. 403)

    a. self-reported typical responses in certain situations

    b. nonverbal behavior in the interview situation and self-reports of his or her typical responses in certain situations

    c. speech patterns and other responses to the interview situation

    d. none of the above

9. Differences in the responses of Type A and Type B individuals are most likely to emerge in situations that (ref. p. 404)

    a. are extremely competitive and controllable

    b. are moderately competitive and uncontrollable

    c. require a short reaction time and quick responses

    d. call for endurance and a narrow focus of attention

10. Compared to Type Bs, Type A individuals (ref. p. 404)

    a. work harder and at a faster pace but do not work longer and more discretionary hours

    b. may have trouble coping in situations that require a narrow focus of attention

    c. experience more satisfaction with their careers

    d. have higher occupational mobility and achieve more

11. The Type A behavior pattern in women correlates positively with (ref. p. 404)

    a. anger

    b. hostility

    c. a masculine sex-role orientation

    d. all of the above

12. Higher levels of hostility have been found among (ref. p. 404)

    a. men

    b. non-Whites

    c. people low in socioeconomic status (SES)

    d. all of the above

13. Cardiovascular reactivity appears to be related to the (ref. p. 405)

   a. chronic experience of anger without expressing it

   <u>b.</u> overt behavioral expression of anger

   c. presence of cynical hostility in both men and women

   d. none of the above

14. Hostility has been traced to (ref. p. 405)

   a. an oppositional orientation toward others

   b. child-rearing patterns characterized by interference and punitiveness

   c. family environments that are nonsupportive and high in conflict

   <u>d.</u> all of the above

15. Individuals who are high in hostility (ref. p. 406)

   a. have chronically higher blood pressure

   b. show more pronounced heart rate reactivity to laboratory stressors

   <u>c.</u> show more pronounced physiological reactions in response to interpersonal stressors

   d. all of the above

16. Negative emotions may be risk factors for CHD due to their relationship with (ref. p. 407)

   a. cardiovascular reactivity

   b. health-compromising behaviors

   c. poor adherence to treatment regimes

   <u>d.</u> all of the above

17. Studies (Blumenthal et al., 1991; 1988) assessing the effectiveness of exercise in reducing cardiovascular risk have concluded that aerobic exercise (ref. p. 408)

   a. reduces behavioral reactivity to stress

   b. reduces systolic and diastolic blood pressure

   c. benefits both men and women at risk for coronary heart disease

   <u>d.</u> all of the above

18. Which of the following has **not** been found to be associated with delay before seeking treatment for myocardial infarction? (ref. p. 409)

   a. interpretation of symptoms as mild disorders

   <u>b.</u> having a family member present at the time of the attack

   c. history of angina or diabetes

   d. experiencing an attack during the daytime

19. Beta-blockers are used in cardiac rehabilitation (ref. p. 410)

   a. to activate the parasympathetic nervous system

   <u>b.</u> to resist the effects of sympathetic nervous system stimulation

   c. to control the pain of angina pectoris

   d. when behavioral stress management interventions fail

20. Cardiac rehabilitation programs involve (ref. p. 411)
    a. aerobic exercise
    b. smoking cessation
    c. reduced alcohol consumption
    d. all of the above

21. Depression and anxiety following a myocardial infarction are implicated in (ref. p. 412)
    a. reduced mortality
    b. increased heart variability
    c. impaired autonomic nervous system functioning
    d. all of the above

22. According to studies of recovery from coronary heart disease (Kulik & Mahler, 1993), social support (ref. pp. 412–413)
    a. was most effective when it was provided by the spouse rather than a confidant
    b. became increasingly effective over time as the patient's recovery progressed
    c. was most influential during the six months immediately after hospitalization
    d. none of the above

23. In a study of cardiac invalidism (Taylor et. al, 1985) wives' perceptions of their husbands' cardiac and physical efficiency were highest when they had (ref. p. 413)
    a. been provided information about their husband's medical and psychological condition
    b. observed their husband's performance on a treadmill task
    c. personally experienced the treadmill task themselves
    d. all of the above

24. Cardiac invalidism occurs when (ref. p. 413)
    a. patients and their spouses underestimate the patient's physical abilities
    b. spouses overestimate the extent of disability and are overprotective of the patient
    c. patients malinger in order to reap secondary gains associated with the sick role
    d. patients feel that they are unable to control the stressors in their daily lives

25. Sudden death from heart attack is most likely to occur (ref. p. 414)
    a. at home
    b. at work
    c. on vacation
    d. while the patient is asleep

26. Diastolic pressure is related to (ref. p. 415)
    a. resistance of the blood vessels to blood flow
    b. the amount of force developed during contraction of the heart
    c. the volume of blood leaving the heart
    d. the arteries' elasticity

27. Mild hypertension is (ref. p. 416)

    a. defined by a diastolic pressure consistently between 105 and 119

    b. considered to be essential hypertension

    c. not considered to be a risk factor for other disorders

    <u>d.</u> now considered to be serious enough to warrant early treatment

28. Males are at greater risk for hypertension (ref. p. 416)

    a. across the life span

    <u>b.</u> prior to age 50

    c. after age 50

    d. none of the above

29. According to a study of hypertension risk factors by Ewart (1991), the family environment may foster _____ which may then contribute to hypertension. (ref. p. 416).

    a. negative affectivity

    <u>b.</u> chronic anger

    c. excessive competitiveness

    d. cynical distrust

30. The prevalence of hypertension among lower-income blacks may be traced to (ref. p. 417)

    a. parental histories of hypertension

    b. racial differences in neuropeptide and cardiovascular response to stressors

    c. exposure to chronic environmental stressors

    <u>d.</u> all of the above

31. People diagnosed with hypertension show large blood pressure responses to stressors that require (ref. p. 418)

    a. avoidant coping

    b. active behavioral responses

    <u>c.</u> passive acceptance and active adaptation

    d. none of the above

32. Studies of the relationship of personality factors to hypertension suggest that (ref. p. 419)

    a. personality factors such as suppressed rage are both necessary and sufficient for the development of hypertension

    b. Type A individuals have a greater prevalence of hypertension than do Type Bs

    <u>c.</u> high day-to-day stress—as measured by characteristics of one's environment, the suppression of anger, and minority status—may combine to produce a high rate of hypertension

    d. none of the above

33. Deficits in communication skills may increase risk factors for hypertension because they may (ref. p. 420)
   a. be related to chronic anger and influence its expression
   b. be psychosocial manifestations of the propensity to react to stressful situations with heightened autonomic reactivity
   c. compromise treatment of the disease
   d. all of the above

34. Drug treatments for hypertension (ref. p. 421)
   a. are more effective than dietary modification and exercise
   b. significantly reduce the incidence of coronary artery disease, morbidity, or mortality
   c. show some success in reducing blood pressure without negative side effects
   d. may effectively reduce the complications of hypertension while increasing the risk for coronary heart disease due to enhanced sympathetic nervous system activity

35. Cognitive-behavioral techniques (ref. pp. 421–422)
   a. may substitute for drug treatments, even in cases of severe hypertension
   b. are associated with lower rates of nonadherence than are drug treatments
   c. are typically combined with drug treatment of hypertension
   d. designed to control the expression of anger have been moderately successful in the treatment of hypertension

36. Which of the following strategies would be most successful in addressing the twin problems of nondiagnosis of hypertension and nonadherence to therapy? (ref. p. 423)
   a. providing a convenient station at the local supermarket where shoppers can check their own blood pressure at no cost
   b. educating patients to help them identify stressful situations and the somatic changes that indicate elevated blood pressure
   c. broadcasting public service announcements that graphically portray the health risks of hypertension
   d. educating patients to avoid stressful situations as much as possible

37. The risk factors for stroke (ref. p. 424)
   a. are independent of those for heart disease
   b. decrease with age
   c. are not subject to modification by lifestyle changes
   d. include cigarette smoking

38. Patients with right-brain damage due to stroke typically suffer (ref. p. 425)
   a. communication disorders such as aphasia
   b. impaired performance on cognitive tasks that require the use of short-term memory
   c. difficulty in processing visual feedback
   d. extreme anxiety and depression

39. Aprosodia (ref. p. 425)
   a. involves difficulty in understanding others and expressing oneself
   b. involves difficulty in expressing and comprehending affect
   c. involves difficulty in recognizing individual faces
   d. results from the accumulating effects of small strokes and often mimics the effects of Alzheimer's disease

40. Predictors of depression in stroke patients include (ref. p. 426)
   a. overprotection by a caregiver
   b. site and severity of stroke
   c. lack of meaning in life
   d. all of the above

41. Type I (insulin-dependent) diabetes (ref. p. 425)
   a. develops relatively late in life (after age 40)
   b. accounts for 90% of all diabetics
   c. is the most serious of the two types of diabetes
   d. occurs when the body fails to produce enough insulin

42. Stress has been implicated in (ref. p. 429)
   a. the development of Type I diabetes in individuals with the affected gene
   b. the aggravation of both Type I and Type II diabetes once diagnosed
   c. adverse effects on adherence to diabetic treatment regimens and diet
   d. all of the above

43. _____ have been found to be significant predictors of adherence to diabetic treatment regimens. (ref. p. 430)
   a. Situational factors
   b. Demographic factors
   c. Personality factors
   d. all of the above

44. Which of the following would **best** predict compliance with a diabetic treatment regimen? (ref. pp. 430–431)
   a. the number of persons in the diabetic's social support network
   b. training the diabetic to discriminate when his or her blood glucose level needed to be modified
   c. information explaining the relationship and roles of the components of a self-care regimen
   d. stress management and relaxation training

45. Studies of diabetic control and adherence indicate the best outcomes are found among adolescents who have (ref. p. 433)
   a. individual therapy
   b. family therapy
   c. parents who are actively involved in tasks such as monitoring glucose levels
   d. a dense social support network

Essay Questions

1. Explain the relationship of lifestyle factors to coronary heart disease and cardiac rehabilitation. (ref. pp. 401–403; 409–412)

2. Your coworker is concerned about the two hard-driving managers who head the department. She says "They are both workaholics whose long hours indicate that they're Type A. Both are walking time bombs who re likely to have heart attacks before they're 50." Respond to your coworker's prediction, citing the research on personality, emotion, and CHD in your text. (ref. pp. 403–407)

3. Explain the relationship of stress management, social support, and psychological distress to recovery from myocardial infarction. (ref. pp. 410–413)

4. What ethnic differences have been found in the incidence of hypertension? What racial and psychosocial factors may be implicated in these ethnic differences? (ref. pp. 417–420)

5. Explain why adherence to diabetic treatment programs is so difficult for most people to achieve. (ref. pp. 429–433).

CHAPTER 14
PSYCHONEUROIMMUNOLOGY, AIDS, CANCER, AND ARTHRITIS

Chapter Outline

I. Psychoneuroimmunology

    A.   The Immune System

    B.   Assessing Immunocompetence

    C.   Stress and Immune Functioning

    D.   Academic Stress and Immune Functioning

    E.   Negative Affect and Immune Functioning

    F.   Stress, Immune Functioning, and Interpersonal Relationships

    G.   Coping and Coping Resources as Moderators of the Stress-Immune Functioning Relationship

    H.   Interventions to Enhance Immunocompetence

    I.   The Conditioning of Immunity

    J.   Pathways from Stress to Immunocompromise

II. AIDS in the United States

    A.   Interventions to Reduce Risk Behaviors for AIDS

    B.   Coping with HIV+ Status

    C.   Coping with AIDS

    D.   Factors That Promote Long-Term Survival

    E.   Psychosocial Factors that Affect the Course of AIDS

III. Cancer

    A.   Who Gets Cancer? A Complex Profile

    B.   Psychosocial Factors and Cancer

    C.   Psychosocial Factors and the Course of Cancer

    D.   Mechanisms Linking Stress and Cancer

IV.   Adjusting to Cancer

     A.   Physical Problems

     B.   Psychological Problems

     C.   Types of Rehabilitative Interventions

          1.   Pharmacologic Interventions

          2.   Behavioral Interventions

          3.   Psychotherapeutic Interventions

V.   Arthritis

     A.   Rheumatoid Arthritis

     B.   Osteoarthritis

     C.   Gout

Learning Objectives

1. Describe the nature and function of the immune system.

2. Identify and describe the primary organs of the immune system.

3. Compare and contrast humoral and cell-mediated immunity.

4. Describe two approaches to assessing immunocompetence.

5. Summarize the results of studies relating stress to immune functioning.

6. Summarize the results of studies relating academic stress to immune functioning.

7. Summarize the results of studies relating negative affect to immune functioning.

8. Summarize the results of studies relating interpersonal relationships, stress, and immune functioning.

9. Explain how coping and coping resources moderate the stress-immune functioning relationship.

10. Describe stress management interventions designed to enhance immunocompetence and evaluate their effectiveness.

11. Summarize the results of studies of the classical conditioning of immune responses.

12. Describe the potential pathways by which stress contributes to immunocompromise.

13. Trace the development of the AIDS epidemic, and describe the nature and course of HIV infection.

14. Describe the demographic risk groups for AIDS and the routes of HIV transmission.

15. Summarize the results of studies assessing the prevalence of high-risk behaviors for AIDS.

16. Describe the nature of interventions designed to reduce risk behaviors for AIDS and evaluate their effectiveness.

17. Summarize the results of studies of psychological adjustment and coping with HIV infection and AIDS.

18. Describe the prevalence of negative attitudes toward people with AIDS.

19. Describe the factors that promote long-term survival among people who are HIV+.

20. Explain how psychosocial factors may affect the course of AIDS.

21. Describe the nature of cancer.

22. Describe the demographic risk groups for cancer.

23. Describe the psychosocial factors that affect the initiation and course of cancer.

24. Summarize the results of studies of the relationship between stress and cancer.

25. Describe the physical and psychological problems associated with cancer and the role of coping strategies in dealing with these problems.

26. Describe pharmacologic, behavioral, and psychotherapeutic rehabilitative interventions for cancer and evaluate their effectiveness.

27. Describe the nature of arthritis.

28. Describe the nature of rheumatoid arthritis. Describe the different treatment interventions for rheumatoid arthritis and evaluate their effectiveness.

29. Describe the nature of osteoarthritis, gout, and their self-care regimens.

Lecture Suggestions

Managing Stigma

Two disorders discussed in this chapter, cancer and AIDS, are associated with a significant social stigma. Thus, secondary victimization is often a problem faced by patients diagnosed with these disorders. Goffman's (1963) discussion of the problems of identity management may be discussed within the context of health-related issues. Susman (1994) presents a review of the research investigating illness-related stigma and Muzzin et al. (1994) discuss the stigma experienced by cancer patients and their families. An extremely sensitive case, facial cancer, may provide a useful focus of the discussion (see Koster & Bergsma, 1990). Finally, Lawless and colleagues (1996) present interviews with 27 women who discuss their experience with the stigma of HIV infection.

Goffman, E. (1963). Stigma. Englewood Cliffs: Prentice-Hall.
Koster, M. E. T. A., & Bergsma, J. (1990). Problems and coping behaviour of facial cancer patients. Social Science and Medicine, 30, 569–578.
Lawless, S., Kippax, S., & Crawford, J. (1996). Dirty, diseased, and undeserving: The positioning of HIV positive women. Social Science and Medicine, 43, 1371–1377.
Muzzin, L. J., Anderson, N. J., Figueredo, A. T., & Gudelis, S. O. (1994). The experience of cancer. Social Science and Medicine, 38, 1201–1208.
Susman, J. (1994). Disability, stigma, and deviance. Social Science and Medicine, 38, 15–22.

Women and AIDS

A discussion of the effects of AIDS on women is useful in emphasizing the fact that AIDS is related to high-risk behaviors rather than to identification with a certain group. Ickovics and Rodin (1992) present recent epidemiological data. Campbell (1990) discusses heterosexual transmission of AIDS and special problems faced by women who are diagnosed with AIDS, as well as women who are caregivers for AIDS patients (see also Hackl et al., 1997).

Campbell, C. (1990). Women and AIDS. Social Science and Medicine, 30, 407–415.

Ickovics, J. R., & Rodin, J. (1992). Women and AIDS in the United States: Epidemiology, natural history, and mediating mechanisms. Health Psychology, 11, 1–16.

Hackl, K. L., Somlai, A. M., Kelly, J. A., & Kalichman, S. C. (1997). Women living with HIV/AIDS: The dual challenge of being a patient and caregiver. Health and Social Work, 22, 53–62.

Exercises, Projects, and Activities

AIDS Education

Perhaps one of the most relevant classroom activities would be to invite a guest speaker for a frank discussion of HIV transmission and high-risk sexual behaviors. Knowledgeable speakers may usually be recruited from public health organizations. Student counseling centers also may have speakers available who are trained in conducting workshops in communication-skills training that specifically target sexual behavior and STDs.

AIDS and Sexual Behavior

Have students write essays that describe the manner in which they would approach the topic of AIDS and STDs within the context of their role as parents providing sex education and counseling to their children. A sample assignment follows.

You are a college-educated parent. You realize you and your two children, Joe (aged 11) and Clara (aged 13), should discuss matters related to birth control and sexuality. However, you also would like to discuss HIV transmission and infection. Write an essay that describes your discussion with your children. Make sure you include examples of high-risk behaviors, as well as behaviors associated with safer sex.

Life-Threatening Illness and Identity Management

The text argues that one of the most distressing aspects of chronic, advancing, and terminal disease is the threat to one's self and identity. The cancer research discussed in this chapter most clearly raises these issues. Have students write an essay discussing the relationship between identity management, illness, and coping. This assignment might also be used as an integrative final exam question.

Recommended Reading

Goffman, E. (1963). Stigma. Englewood Cliffs: Prentice-Hall.

This easy-to-read book describes people's attempts to manage their spoiled identities that result from being stigmatized by others due to diagnoses of certain illnesses, facial disfigurement, etc.

Levy, J. A., Jasmin, C., Bez, Gabriel (Eds.) (1997). <u>Cancer, AIDS, and quality of life</u>. New York: Plenum.

This volume focuses on issues of long-term survivorship and quality of life among people with cancer and AIDS. Chapters address psychosocial issues as well as treatment interventions.

Saphier, D. (1993). Psychoimmunology: The missing links. In J. Schulkin (Ed.), <u>Hormonally induced changes in mind and brain</u> (pp. 191-224). San Diego: Academic Press.

This chapter reviews the basic principles of psychoimmunology. It discusses psychosomatic interactions, the effects of stress on immune functioning, the relationship between the nervous, endocrine, and immune systems, etc.

Shilts, R. (1988). <u>And the band played on: Politics, people and the AIDS epidemic</u>. New York: Penguin.

This controversial book presents the argument that homophobia, lack of political direction, and a delayed response by public health administrators have exacerbated the transmission of AIDS among the American population.

Winiarski, M. G. (Ed.) (1997). <u>HIV mental health for the 21st century</u>. New York: New York University Press.

The intended audience for this book is mental health practitioners. Many chapters, however, address topics relevant to health psychology including secondary prevention interventions, models of medical care, program evaluation, etc. The appendix is an up-to-date list of sources for additional information.

True-False Questions

1. T <u>F</u> Humoral immunity operates at the cellular level and is mediated by T lymphocytes. (ref. p. 436)

2. <u>T</u> F Studies with human and animal subjects indicate that exposure to stressors is related to immunologic change. (ref. p. 437)

3. T <u>F</u> Studies have found impaired immune functioning among bereaved individuals, even if these individuals do not show evidence of depression. (ref. p. 440)

4. <u>T</u> F Impaired immune functioning has been found in samples of adults who have experienced short-term marital conflict, marital separation, and divorce. (ref. p. 441)

5. T <u>F</u> Corticosteroids have both an immunosuppressive and immunoenhancing effect under different conditions. (ref. p. 444)

6. <u>T</u> F A person may test HIV-seropositive (HIV+) but be free of a diagnosis of AIDS for years. (ref. p. 445)

7. <u>T</u> F Past sexual practice is an important predictor of AIDS-related risk behaviors. (ref. p. 451)

8. T <u>F</u> The AIDS epidemic has led to increased candor and willingness to volunteer information about one's sexual history, especially among college students. (ref. p. 454)

9. <u>T</u>   F   Japanese-American women are more susceptible to breast cancer the longer they have lived in the United States and the more they have adopted the American culture. (ref. p. 460)

10.   T   <u>F</u>   The most prevalent of the autoimmune diseases is cancer. (ref. p. 470)

Multiple-Choice Questions

1.   Which of the following is **not** one of the lymphoid organs of the immune system? (ref. p. 436)

   <u>a</u>.   the skin

   b.   the spleen

   c.   the tonsils

   d.   bone marrow

2.   Natural killer cells (ref. p. 436)

   a.   recognize, ingest, and destroy antigens

   b.   contribute to inflammatory and allergic reactions

   c.   assist in the activation of T cells through the secretion of cytokine

   <u>d</u>.   secrete interferon and attack and destroy cells infected by viruses

3.   T lymphocytes (ref. p. 436)

   a.   play an important role in humoral immunity

   b.   confer immunity by the production and secretion of antibodies

   <u>c</u>.   secrete chemicals that kill invading organisms and infected cells

   d.   release antibodies into the blood

4.   Helper T (T_H) cells (ref. p. 436)

   a.   respond to specific antigens

   <u>b</u>.   enhance the function of T_C cells, B cells and macrophages by producing lymphokines

   c.   produce lymphokines that suppress immune activity

   d.   produce immunoglobulins, which are the basis of antigen-specific reactions

5.   Indicators of immune functioning are (ref. p. 437)

   a.   highly correlated

   b.   highly reliable

   c.   unaffected by personal activities and events

   <u>d</u>.   none of the above

6.   Herbert and Cohen reviewed 38 studies relating stress to human immune functioning. They concluded that (ref. p. 437)

   a.   subjective reports of stress were related to larger changes in functional immune measures than were objectively-determined events

   b.   long-term naturalistic stressors increase the number of circulating suppressor/cytotoxic T cells and natural killer cells

   <u>c</u>.   stress is related to decreases in measures of immune functioning

   d.   all of the above

7. Stress has been related to (ref. p. 438)
    a. rates of infectious disease in children and adults
    b. the development of herpes virus infections
    c. altered immunologic functioning and susceptibility to immune-related disorders in animals
    <u>d.</u> all of the above

8. Academic stress has been associated with (ref. p. 440)
    <u>a.</u> decreases in total T, T_H, and T_S lymphocytes
    b. increases in natural killer cells
    c. higher rates of infectious disease in adults but not children
    d. increased distress but few changes in immune functioning

9. Herbert and Cohen's (1993) review of the literature found support for the notion that immune functioning is impaired by (ref. p. 440)
    a. negative affectivity
    b. anxiety
    <u>c.</u> depression
    d. hostility

10. Premature maternal separation may have adverse effects on the immune system of rats due to (ref. p. 440)
    a. impaired nutrition
    b. disturbed hypothalamic functioning
    c. poor maturation of the immune system
    <u>d.</u> all of the above

11. The quality of one's interpersonal relationships has been implicated in immunocompromise. Which of the following has **not** been found to be associated with physical and emotional illness? (ref. p. 440)
    <u>a.</u> being single
    b. bereavement
    c. short-term marital conflict
    d. divorce and separation

12. Long-term provision of care to friends or family members with long-term illness has been linked with a range of health-related problems. This can be attributed to caregivers' (ref. p. 441)
    a. poor health habits
    b. disrupted sleep patterns
    <u>c.</u> experience of severe, long-term stressors
    d. all of the above

13. Studies of personality and coping styles have found that the stress-immune functioning relationship is moderated by (ref. pp. 441–442)
    a. optimism
    b. active coping strategies
    c. perceived control
    <u>d.</u> all of the above

14. According to Bandura (1989), perceived self-efficacy may (ref. p. 442)
    a. directly reduce the experience of stress
    b. reduce the tendency to develop depression in response to stressful events
    c. modulate immunologic reactivity via the central nervous system
    <u>d.</u> all of the above

15. An experimental study of the effects of controllable versus uncontrollable noise on natural killer cell activity (Sieber et al., 1992) found (ref. p. 442)
    a. perceived control moderated the short-term effects of stress on the immune system
    b. perceived control moderated the long-term effects of stress on the immune system
    c. desire for control and dispositional optimism enhanced the negative impact of uncontrollable noise
    <u>d.</u> all of the above

16. Immunocompetence has been found to be enhanced by (ref. p. 443)
    <u>a.</u> relaxation training
    b. social contact
    c. repressing one's thoughts about the stressful event
    d. stress management skills

17. HIV affects primarily (ref. p. 445)
    <u>a.</u> helper T cells and macrophages
    b. leukocytes
    c. natural killer cells
    d. B cells

18. The time between progression from HIV+ status to a diagnosis of AIDS is most strongly influenced by (ref. p. 446)
    a. individual differences
    <u>b.</u> socioeconomic factors
    c. sexual orientation
    d. ethnicity

19. Early detection of HIV+ status may be especially important due to the impact of _____ on the progression of AIDS. (ref. p. 446)
    a. lifestyle factors
    b. experimental drug treatments such as AZT
    c. general health status
    <u>d.</u> all of the above

20. The most promising development in the treatment of AIDS is (ref. p. 448)
    a. an HIV vaccine
    b. AZT
    <u>c.</u> protease inhibitors
    d. DDI

21. According to the Centers for Disease Control, the numbers of AIDS cases are growing fastest among (ref. p. 449)

    a. ethnic minorities

    b. gay men

    c. minority women

    d. IV drug users

22. Studies of high-risk behaviors with respect to AIDS indicate that little behavior change has been found among (ref. p. 449)

    a. drug users

    b. urban minorities

    c. adolescents and young adults

    d. all of the above

23. Interventions designed to provide knowledge about AIDS and routes of transmission would be **most** effective with (ref. p. 450)

    a. older gay men

    b. younger gay men

    c. minority inner-city adolescents

    d. younger, middle-class adults

24. Perceptions of self-efficacy have been related to (ref. p. 451)

    a. frequency of condom use

    b. number of sexual partners

    c. number of anonymous sexual partners

    d. all of the above

25. Condom use among adolescents (ref. p. 453)

    a. appears to be decreasing

    b. is independent of other behavioral problems such as drug and alcohol use

    c. has been found to be related to peer norms and perceptions of personal efficacy

    d. all of the above

26. Testing seropositive for the HIV virus has been found to be associated with (ref. p. 455)

    a. elevated levels of social and emotional impairment

    b. both short-term and long-term increases in psychological distress

    c. difficulties in adjustment and coping because it leaves individuals in a state of threat but without a specific stressor to combat

    d. none of the above

27. Fear of AIDS and negative reactions toward people with AIDS have been documented among (ref. p. 455)

    a. homophobic persons

    b. people who fear contagion

    c. medical practitioners

    d. all of the above

28. Evaluations of interventions with populations at risk for HIV infection suggest that such programs (ref. p. 454)
   a. have little effect in the reduction of HIV risk-related behavior
   b. should focus on high-risk sexual activity and condom use
   c. will need to be tailored to the specific age and ethnic group targeted
   d. all of the above

29. Studies of the relationship of attributions that AIDS patients make for the cause of their disease and their psychosocial adjustment suggest that (ref. p. 456)
   a. attributing the cause of AIDS to oneself may be associated with depression and anxiety
   b. self-blame is relatively infrequent
   c. most gay men living with AIDS felt that their promiscuous sexual behavior caused the disorder
   d. all of the above

30. According to the research cited in your text, which of the following patients would be expected to be better adjusted and most successful in coping with AIDS? (ref. p. 456)
   a. Paul, who is confident that the medical personnel who staff his experimental treatment program are outstanding in the field and his best chance for survival
   b. Mary, who contracted AIDS through a transfusion and feels that she has no personal control over the disease
   c. Tom, who has turned to alternatives to traditional medicine and feels that his holistic practitioner can best arrest the progression of the disorder
   d. John, who feels that he can control the disease and its symptoms and has taken personal responsibility for its treatment

31. One factor that seems to distinguish long-term survivors of AIDS is (ref. p. 458)
   a. coping style
   b. physical exercise
   c. self-efficacy
   d. stress management

32. Which of the following has **not** been found to contribute to positive adjustment and long-term survival among people with AIDS? (ref. p. 458)
   a. ability to find meaning in being HIV+
   b. concealing one's sexual orientation and HIV status
   c. social support
   d. optimism

33. All cancers result from (ref. p. 459)
   a. immunocompromise
   b. a dysfunction in RNA
   c. a dysfunction in DNA
   d. a reduction in DNA

34. Studies of the development of cancer across species indicate that (ref. p. 460)
    a. there is little between-species variability
    b. there is little within-species variability
    c. some subgroups within a species may be more susceptible to certain cancers than others
    d. none of the above

35. The fact that many cancers run in families may be explained by (ref. p. 460)
    a. a genetically inherited predisposition to cancer
    b. lifestyle factors that may influence the development of cancer
    c. ethnic differences in the development of certain cancers
    d. all of the above

36. Carcinogens are (ref. p. 461)
    a. substances that cross the placenta and cause fetal abnormalities
    b. substances that are implicated in the development of cancer
    c. behavioral factors that influence the course of cancer development
    d. dietary factors that influence the course of cancer development

37. Research investigating the relationship between personality traits and cancer has found (ref. p. 462)
    a. a positive association between cancer and emotional repression
    b. a positive association between cancer and depression
    c. no relationship between psychosocial variables and depression
    d. all of the above; research to date is inconclusive

38. Stress may be linked to cancer via which of the following mechanisms? (ref. p. 464)
    a. immunocompromise
    b. impaired DNA repair
    c. NK cell activity
    d. all of the above

39. The consequence of receiving chemotherapy in the same place by the same person under the same circumstances is (ref. p. 465)
    a. conditioned nausea
    b. conditioned immune suppression
    c. impaired long-term compliance
    d. all of the above

40. A study of cancer patients conducted by Dunkel-Schetter and her colleagues (1992) found that patients who coped with their cancer-related problems via _____ showed more emotional distress. (ref. p. 466)
    a. social support
    b. cognitive escape-avoidant strategies
    c. distancing
    d. none of the above

41. A number of interventions have been employed to facilitate cancer patients' coping with chemotherapy. Which of the following interventions has been found to be **least** effective? (ref. p.468)

    a. relaxation

    b. guided imagery

    c. biofeedback

    d. distraction

42. Peer counseling groups, such as Reach to Recovery, involve (ref. p. 469)

    a. groups of patients with the same disorder who discuss common issues and problems

    b. a well-adjusted patient acting as an adviser to a newly diagnosed patient

    c. a well-adjusted patient counseling the newly diagnosed patient's family in social support skills

    d. one-on-one intensive psychotherapy

43. Rheumatoid arthritis (ref. p. 470)

    a. is the least crippling form of arthritis

    b. strikes primarily middle-aged and elderly adults

    c. has been associated with a perfectionistic and depressed personality type

    d. is relatively unaffected by stress and psychological variables

44. Osteoarthritis (ref. p. 472)

    a. affects the small joints of the wrists, hands, and feet

    b. involves the destruction of the bone and muscle tissue of the joint

    c. involves the deterioration of cartilage in weight-bearing joints

    d. none of the above

45. Gout (ref. p. 472)

    a. is more prevalent in females than in males

    b. results from the buildup of uric acid in the body

    c. can be managed by maintaining proper weight and taking aspirin

    d. none of the above

Essay Questions

1. Explain how stress is related to immunocompromise. Exactly how does the immune system respond to stress? (ref. pp. 437–438)

2. What is the relationship between depression, loneliness, interpersonal conflict, and immunocompromise? Do individual differences in coping styles affect this relationship? If so, how? (ref. pp. 440–442)

3. Evaluate the effectiveness of interventions to reduce risk behaviors for AIDS. In your opinion, what groups are currently most at risk? Why are these groups so difficult to reach? (ref. pp. 450–455)

4. Your roommate has just confided in you that a friend of hers has tested HIV+. Knowing you are taking a health psychology course, she's asking for advice on two matters. First, she would like to have any information that might be helpful in understanding how to help her friend cope. Second, she would like to know what to expect in terms of her friend's medical condition. How long do people live with HIV? What factors influence prognoses? (ref. pp. 455–459)

5. How do psychosocial factors influence the initiation and course of cancer? (ref. pp. 461–464)

CHAPTER 15
HEALTH PSYCHOLOGY: CHALLENGES FOR THE FUTURE

Chapter Outline

I.   Health Promotion

II.   Stress and Its Management

III.   Use of Health Services

IV.   Management of Serious Illness

V.   Trends for the Future

        A.   The Changing Nature of Medical Practice

        B.   Systematic Documentation of Treatment Effectiveness

        C.   Systematic Documentation of Cost-Effectiveness

        D.   Remaining Issues

        E.   Becoming a Health Psychologist

Learning Objectives

1. Summarize the research agenda of health psychology.

2. Describe the goals of health psychology research in health promotion, including the shift of focus from mortality to morbidity, the role of environmental hazards which may pose health risks, and changes in medical practice and research.

3. Describe the goals of health psychology research in stress and its management, including populations at risk, the psychophysiology of stress, and social support.

4. Describe the goals of health psychology research in the use of health services, including health care reform and the provision of state-of-the-art care.

5. Describe the goals of health psychology research in patient-practitioner communication, including trends in medical education and care.

6. Describe the goals of health psychology research in pain management.

7. Describe the goals of health psychology research in chronic illness.

8. Describe the goals of health psychology research in the management of terminal illness, including the impact of the AIDS epidemic.

9. Describe the goals of health psychology research in the development of coronary heart disease, hypertension, stroke, diabetes, AIDS, cancer, and arthritis.

10. Summarize the changing nature of medical practice and technology. Describe the comprehensive intervention model.

11. Explain the role of health psychology in the systematic documentation of treatment effectiveness and cost-effectiveness.

12. Describe the training requirements for health psychologists and the areas in which they are employed.

Lecture Suggestions

Health Psychology in the 21st Century

The topics in Chapter 15 may be expanded by presenting Belar's (1997) Division of Health Psychology Presidential Address in which she discusses trends in clinical health psychology. In addition, Chesney (1993) discusses five trends in health psychology: early identification of at-risk individuals, increasing expectations of successful behavior change programs, growing populations of persons coping with chronic illness, shifts to community and public health perspectives, and the need to treat problems on a global scale. These issues are discussed within the context of HIV infection.

Belar, C. D. (1997). Clinical health psychology: A specialty for the 21st century. Health Psychology, 16, 411–416.

Chesney, M. A. (1993). Health psychology in the 21st century: Acquired immunodeficiency syndrome as a harbinger of things to come. Health Psychology, 12, 259–268.

Women's Health Initiative

As has been mentioned throughout the text, medical research on women's health is sorely lacking in some areas. A recent article by Matthews et al. (1997) describes the design and protocols and provides a summary of the current status of the Women's Health Initiative, a 15-year study of 164,500 postmenopausal women funded by the NIH.

Matthews, K. A., Shumaker, S. A., Bowen, D. J., Langer, R. D., Hunt, J. R., Kaplan, R. M., Klesges, R. C., & Ritenbaugh, C. (1997). Women's Health Initiative: Why now? What is it? What's new? American Psychologist, 52, 101–116.

Recommended Reading

Gallant, S. J., Keita, G. P., & Royak-Schaler, R. (Eds.) (1997) Health care for women: Psychological, social, and behavioral influences. Washington, DC: American Psychological Association.

This edited volume presents a biopsychosocial perspective on current and future research in women's health issues. Topics include gender and aging, stress, coronary heart disease, and cancer.

Kato, P. M., & Mann, T. (Eds.) (1996). <u>Handbook of diversity issues in health psychology</u>. New York: Plenum.

The changing demographics of the United States and related health concerns are the focus of this volume. Chapters focus on health psychology across the life-span and the influence of gender, sexual orientation, and ethnicity on physical and mental health.

True-False Questions

1. T   <u>F</u>   Americans have made substantial gains in changing poor health habits including reduced consumption of high-cholesterol, high-fat foods and alcoholic beverages. (ref. p. 476)

2. T   F   To date, research has yet to establish the effectiveness of behavioral immunization programs that address health habits such as smoking, drug abuse, and diet. (ref. p. 477)

3. <u>T</u>   F   According to Kaplan (1989), mortality is currently overemphasized relative to morbidity. (ref. p. 478)

4. T   <u>F</u>   Some research suggests that because men and women differ in their biochemistry, smoking may be only half as hazardous for women as for men. (ref. p. 481)

5. <u>T</u>   F   The health needs of vulnerable populations (e.g., children and the poor) should be afforded special priority in the study of stress and its reduction. (ref. p. 483)

6. T   <u>F</u>   Most surveys suggest that patients want less expensive high-technology medical treatment, except in the terminal phase of illness. (ref. p. 484)

7. <u>T</u>   F   The demographics of people with AIDS is shifting to ethnic minorities, women, and the poor. (ref. p. 486)

8. <u>T</u>   F   As medicine becomes technologically more complex, the use of control-enhancing interventions will become even more important. (ref. p. 488)

9. T   <u>F</u>   The issue of treatment effectiveness is becoming less urgent as behavioral and psychological interventions have become well established in managed health care systems. (ref. p. 490)

10. <u>T</u>   F   DRGs eventually may restrict the behavioral treatment of medical disorders because they fall outside the time period in the treatment guidelines. (ref. p. 490)

Multiple-Choice Questions

1. In general, the health habits of most Americans have _____ over the last 15 to 20 years. (ref. p. 476)
   <u>a.</u> improved
   b. remained unchanged
   c. become more variable
   d. worsened

2. According to the text, over the past 15 to 20 years, Americans' alcohol consumption has _____ and exercise has _____. (ref. p. 476)

   a. decreased; increased
   b. increased; decreased
   c. remained unchanged; decreased
   d. remained unchanged; increased

3. In the future, health promotion interventions will most likely target (ref. p. 476)

   a. the schools
   b. the community
   c. the workplace
   d. any of the above

4. Early drug prevention programs, such as DARE, are an example of (ref. p. 477)

   a. cost containment
   b. behavioral immunization
   c. cost effectiveness
   d. patient consumerism

5. Health promotion programs that target the elderly (ref. p. 477)

   a. are a waste of money since health habits are established early in life
   b. are important right now, but they will become less important as the size of the elderly cohort declines over the next 20 years
   c. will become increasingly important as the size of the elderly cohort continues to increase over the next 20 years
   d. will become less important since the elderly cohort is an exceptionally healthy and active one

6. Significant gains in the quality of life would best be achieved by reorienting the focus of health promotion toward (ref. p. 478)

   a. reducing the period of morbidity
   b. delaying mortality
   c. early identification of risk factors
   d. all of the above

7. Refocusing health promotion strategies toward morbidity should (ref. p. 478)

   a. reduce health care costs
   b. enhance quality of life
   c. also take into consideration socioeconomic differences in health and health care
   d. all of the above

8. As the text notes, behavior modification efforts should target risk factors that account for the greatest degree of morbidity. By this criterion, which of the following interventions has the greatest potential benefit? (ref. p. 478).

   a. smoking cessation and prevention programs
   b. programs to lower cholesterol
   c. weight reduction programs
   d. any of the above would be equally effective

9. Unhealthy environments have been linked to (ref. p. 480)
   a. mental health problems
   b. physical health problems
   c. conflictual or abusive interpersonal relationships
   d. all of the above

10. Health care in the United States is becoming (ref. p. 480)
   a. increasingly egalitarian
   b. more accessible to the poor, but the number of middle-class households without health insurance is increasing
   c. increasingly oriented toward health promotion and primary prevention
   d. a two-tiered system

11. Women (ref. p. 481)
   a. live on average 5 years longer than men
   b. are sick more often than men
   c. are decreasing their use of health-compromising substances
   d. all of the above

12. Heart disease research has substantially overrepresented (ref. p. 481)
   a. men
   b. women
   c. the elderly
   d. minorities

13. The American female population is (ref. pp. 481–483)
   a. sick more frequently than the male population
   b. increasing its consumption of alcohol and cigarettes
   c. increasingly called on to become caregivers for elderly parents
   d. all of the above

14. One important characteristic of the dual-career family which has an important impact upon primary prevention for stress-related disorders is the fact that (ref. p. 483)
   a. nutrition in dual-career households is generally poor
   b. the dual-career family has less time for meeting social support needs
   c. working wives and mothers show problems in psychological adjustment
   d. all of the above

15. In order to be more effective in providing social support, self-help groups must (ref. p. 484)
   a. prove to be cost-effective
   b. be supplemented with traditional psychotherapy
   c. incorporate more treatment modalities in their formats
   d. broaden their appeal more generally for the population

16. Which of the following is **not** one of the three basic problems facing the health care system in the United States? (ref. p. 484)
    a. Health care costs too much.
    b. The system is inequitable.
    c. Third-party providers have failed to act responsibly.
    d. Many consumers make inappropriate use of the system.

17. The most significant change in American health care that has implications for health psychology is (ref. p. 484)
    a. the expense of high technology
    b. trends in physician education
    c. the rapid growth of managed care
    d. patient consumerism

18. Trends within medical care suggest that the problem of patient-practitioner communication is likely to (ref. p. 485)
    a. improve
    b. worsen
    c. hamper physician's efforts to find cost-effectiveness treatments
    d. become less important than cost-containment

19. Improvements in the technology of pain control have led to (ref. p. 485)
    a. increased use of improved pharmacological pain control techniques
    b. a shift in the responsibility for pain control from the practitioner to the patient
    c. increased acceptance of comanagement of pain by the practitioner and the patient
    d. state-of-the-art treatments for chronic pain becoming increasingly available at local clinics and hospitals

20. Future programs targeting the management of chronic illness must incorporate (ref. p. 485)
    a. cost-effective interventions to improve quality of life
    b. assessment of needs in all domains of life during the acute period of illness
    c. regular needs assessment over the long term to identify potential problems
    d. all of the above

21. Which of the following is **not** a focus of investigations of the psychological aspects of terminal illness? (ref. p. 486)
    a. ethical issues surrounding death and dying
    b. changing public attitudes about death and dying
    c. meeting the needs of family members
    d. the unique problems faced by AIDS patients

22. As the elderly population increases, a corresponding increase is expected in the incidence of (ref. p. 487)
    a. acute, but life-threatening, disorders
    b. Type A behavior
    c. chronic disorders
    d. Alzheimer's disease

23. Comprehensive intervention models (ref. p. 488)

    a. concentrate and coordinate medical and psychological expertise
    b. have yet to be developed for chronic diseases
    c. have proven to be less expensive than other models and remarkably cost effective
    d. all of the above

24. Which of the following interventions has the **least** amount of documentation supporting its claims of cost-effectiveness? (ref. p. 491)

    a. enhanced perceptions of control
    b. training practitioners in effective communication
    c. chronic pain management
    d. none of the above

25. The current trend toward cost containment pushes the field in the direction of research questions designed to (ref. pp. 490–491)

    a. assess the efficacy of self-help groups and self-management programs to provide services to people who otherwise would not receive care
    b. keep patients out of the health care system
    c. lower the costs of providing health care services
    d. all of the above

26. Most health psychologists work in (ref. p. 495)

    a. private practice
    b. hospitals and clinics
    c. universities and other academic settings
    d. governmental agencies

Essay Questions

1. Choose one of the health-related behaviors that has been covered in the text (e.g., smoking, alcohol consumption, etc.). Using this behavior as your example, explain how research in health psychology can make a contribution to health promotion in the United States and abroad. (ref. pp. 476–481)

2. Explain the role of health psychology within the context of health care reform in the United States. (ref. pp. 484–485)

3. Explain what is meant by comprehensive intervention models. What contributions might a team of health psychologists make to health care delivery under this model? (ref. pp. 488–489)

4. Explain current pressures toward cost containment of health care costs. In what ways do these economic factors affect research and practice in health psychology? (ref. pp. 489–492)